From Dawn Until Dusk

From Dawn Until Dusk

Burl A. Jones

Montana
2010

Copyright © 2010 by Burl A. Jones
All rights reserved.

ISBN-13: 978-0-9828601-0-6

Manufactured in the United States of America
First Edition

Published in the United States by

Bangtail Press
P. O. Box 11262
Bozeman, MT 59719
www.bangtailpress.com

All illustrations by Burl A. Jones
Book design by Allen Morris Jones
Cover photo by Dr. David Santrock
Photo on page eight, "Flat Lake," by Dr. Mark S. Jones

To my long-suffering, patient, and tolerant partner, Euni; my wife, to whom I owe more than words can say.

Contents

Foreword *11*
Introduction *13*

Part I

A Quick Sketch of a Life *17*

Part II

Ol' Enik *33*
West Virginia Deer Hunting *37*
Persistence *43*
Mother Nature's Child *47*
Goat Cliffs *57*
A Narrow escape *65*
Sometimes the Bear *70*
Back to Montana *76*
What the Magpies Said *85*
The Far North *89*
A Black Wolf in British Columbia *103*
A Buck and a Bull for the Boys *113*
Mark the Hunter *117*
An Unexpected Blizzard *122*
Another Elk for Allen *129*
Mountain Lions in Montana *133*
Alaska Caribou *138*
Dall Sheep in Northwest Territories *150*
Sheep, Moose, and Bear in British Columbia *159*
Someday *167*

Part III

Foreign Lands *176*
Mozambique, by Dr. Mark S. Jones *178*
Montana Horns, by Allen Morris Jones *186*

Foreword

by Allen Morris Jones

You can't choose your own childhood, no more than you can choose your native language or the color of your eyes. We all come into the world burdened or blessed with a portfolio of givens. No sooner are you wiped off dry than you're shoved off into the deep end, sink or swim.

My brother and I, in this respect, have been very lucky indeed. Our mother, a little red-haired firecracker, a talented singer and gifted potter, makes it a matter of policy to go through life unintimidated. She takes a situation and tells it what to do. And Dad, an acclaimed artist and sportsman, has always been most comfortable outside, working, fishing, and hunting. Between them, they've given us the best possible road map for how to live our lives.

Among Dad's thousand gifts, I've come to value most the example of his enthusiasm, his passion for things. He raised us in the woods, and so taught us, from an early age, to shoot and skin and track. In a world increasingly filled with cold concrete and loud noise, he gave us a sense of groundedness. Here, son, here's how things really work. Fox squirrels in West Virginia or Cape buffalo in Africa, this is the way energy travels from meat

From Dawn Until Dusk

to mouth, how some animals die to be eaten while others eat to live. You can regret it but you can't change it. You can only show your respect. Every new experience, every day in the field with Dad, has been another gift, another jewel to thread onto the long strings of our lives.

Like most truly happy men, Dad is also generous. He wants to share what he has. In these pages, you'll find a few life lessons and a few hard truths. Some sticky situations and some warm, heartfelt moments. But most of all you'll find the spirit of a man who wants to give a little bit of himself. I for one am grateful for the experiences, for the lessons, and for this book.

Introduction

Burl A. Jones

Growing up in rural West Virginia in the fifties, I was relatively innocent by today's standards. Drugs were unknown, crime was always somewhere else, and most families stayed intact. Guns were honored and hunting was respected. In the fall our biggest dilemma was finding time for both football and hunting. I aspired to be not only the best football player I could be but also the best hunter. That meant, in some measure, going west.

As I have grown older, the adventures I had in my youth have come to take on undue importance. And while my early dreams of being able to hunt, fish, and hike in the exotic and wild places of the world have largely come true, some part of me—the child hunting squirrels in West Virginia, maybe—still finds it hard to believe that it was *me* that did those things; a kid from West Virginia who actually shot sheep in Canada and bears in Russia.

The stories in the following pages are just a few of the adventures I've shared with my family and friends. These experiences have provided the inspiration for my extensive work in taxidermy and fine art sculpture. Sadly, many of these adventures would not be possible today, given changing regulations and opportunities.

I wrote this book hoping to share some of the excitement I

From Dawn Until Dusk

felt in my hunts, and continue to feel, waiting for the next big adventure.

Through all of this, through whatever accomplishments I've enjoyed, none of it would have been possible without the help and support of my lifetime partner, Euni. And so many of my adventures would have been less enjoyable if I hadn't been able to share them with my sons, Mark and Allen.

I hope you find something here that you enjoy as well.

Part I

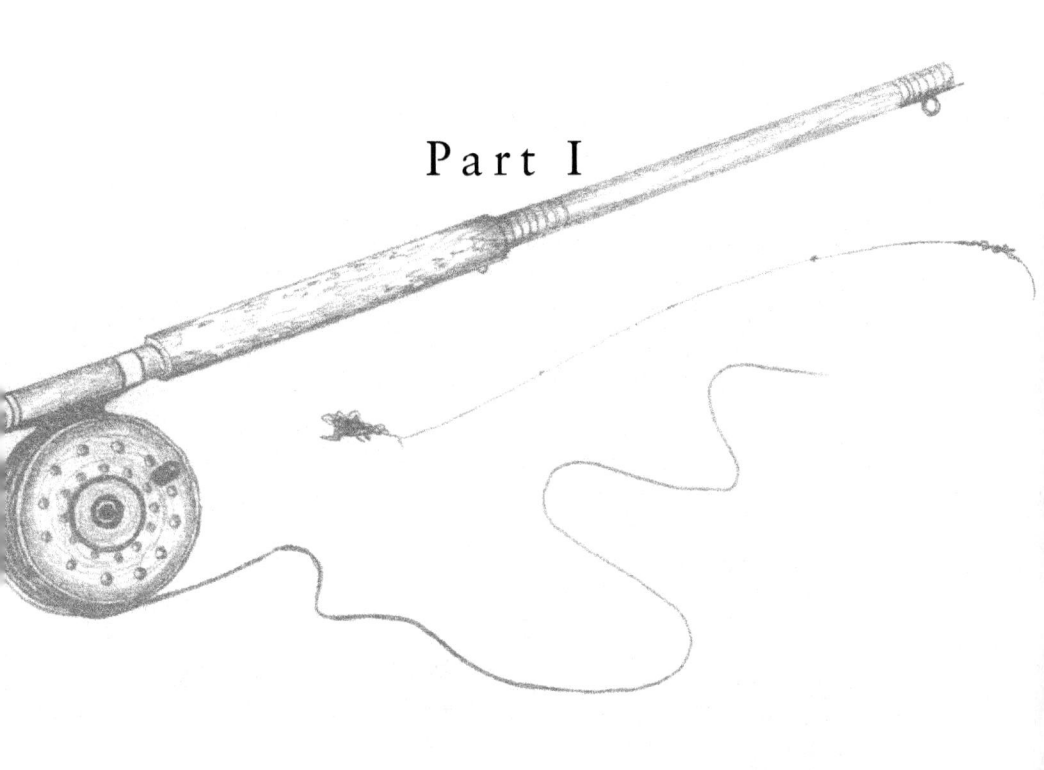

From Dawn Until Dusk

Burl Jones, above, with two early trophies, a Rocky Mountain bighorn sheep and an Alberta moose.

Left, Burl as a fourteen-year-old football player, on his way to making all state a few years later in high school.

A Quick Sketch of a Life

It seems that one's life is largely controlled by those that came before and the decisions they made.

For me, the decision of my ancestors to settle and farm in the hills of West Virginia instead of moving farther west to the fertile plains or mountains shaped me in ways I can only begin to imagine.

My mother's family was German; her maiden name was Bumgardner. My great-grandfather acquired one thousand acres on the Middle Fork of the Poca River in Jackson County at one dollar an acre. He later divided this property among his children. My grandfather, Howard Bumgardner, owned and made his living on 170 acres of the best of the original thousand.

Howard was a tall and lean man with a puritan's stern demeanor. A hardworking farmer with pride in his registered Herefords and well kept fields, he and his family lived a Spartan life. Grandmother was a very small, timid woman who seemed quite content to work as cook, housemaid, and mother to her brood. Her maiden name was Duff, daughter of Major Duff and Amentia Fisher. My mother, Mary, was the third of nine children (three sons and six daughters).

From Dawn Until Dusk

I remember the Duffs somewhat, as they lived into their nineties on a small hilltop farm near Kenna in Jackson County, West Virginia. Great-grandpa Duff was a small, wiry man, and well known as a colorful character.

I never knew any of Grandpa Bumgardner's ancestors, but his parents were Charles Bumgardner and Ann Fisher. He had no brothers and only two sisters. The only sister I knew was Hettie, who married Oren Garnes and lived into her nineties.

Mother's siblings were all of average size and above average intelligence. Mother was the first to die, at age eighty, after suffering from chronic, lymphatic leukemia for sixteen years. She was a gentle yet strong woman—loving but not demonstrative. Intelligent but only schooled through the eighth grade in the small one room school near their farm. None of her siblings had further schooling except Raymond who graduated from Sissonville High School at age sixteen.

We paid weekly visits to the farm while Mother's parents lived, and often helped in the summer with haying and gardening. I remember the farm as a wonderful place, with a creek for fishing and swimming, woods for hunting squirrels and rabbits, and a big garden that provided for fall watermelon feasts under huge pear trees. My mother, however, remembered the farm as a place of hard work and tough times. Her childhood dresses were made from feed sacks, and her Christmas presents were candy and an apple. Grandpa was a tough, unsympathetic man, and Mother was glad to leave the farm. She never wanted to return to that kind of life.

On Dad's side I never knew any of his grandparents or even his uncles or aunts, but his parents lived into their seventies and eighties, and I knew them well. Grandmother Jones was a Blackshire, daughter of Greenberry Blackshire. She was born on Camp Creek off Poca River in Jackson County, West Virginia, in 1887. She lived until 1973. A sweet and gentle woman, she was always anxious to feed and care for her grandchildren. She was born in a shack and spent most of her life raising kids, farming a poor hillside farm, and tending a three-room house with a cut-stone pillar foundation (there was lots of room under the porch for the dogs). I know nothing of her early family life but I know she brought two intelligent children into her marriage with

From left, Burl's Grandma Bumgardner, Aunt Pauline, Aunt Helen, his grandfather, and Aunt Midge. Photo, circa 1949.

Sheridan, my grandfather.

Grandma's first two children (Dad's half brother and sister) were William Shouldis and Oakley Harper. With Sheridan she then had Hattie, Harry, Opa (Dad), Lincoln, Francis, Raymond (Jack), and Curtis.

Subsistence farming in those days meant expending great effort to raise corn, beans, tomatoes, fruit, cabbage, and other vegetables. In order to provide sustenance through the winter, everything had to be dried, pickled, canned, or buried. Wood had to be continuously cut, carried, split, and stacked. Hunting was a necessity rather than a pastime. My ancestors ate squirrels, rabbits, opossums, and raccoons. They sold the fur of foxes, muskrats, raccoons, and skunks.

Dad's father, Sheridan, was the son of Emmanuel Jones and Elmira Clarkson (said to be half Cherokee). Emmanuel served under General Sheridan in the civil war, and subsequently named one of his sons Sheridan.

My father and his siblings grew up just upstream of his Grandfather Emmanuel's farm on Higgenbottom creek off the Poca River.

From Dawn Until Dusk

In his younger years, Sheridan, my dad's father, was an abusive and irresponsible husband and father. He gambled, shirked work, and drank to excess. This put a heavy load on Dad, who came to be responsible for many of the duties on the farm. This caused him pain in many ways, both emotionally and physically.

One day in the fall when Dad was only twelve, he was left to tend a horse-drawn cane mill that was grinding cane for molasses. His hand caught in the grinding gear, and he lost one of his fingers and some of the dexterity in his hand. Sheridan felt sorry enough for Dad that he let him continue on to high school rather than stopping his education at eighth grade as he had done with Dad's older siblings.

I knew Grandpa Jones only as a fun-loving old man whom most everyone respected and liked. He was uncle Sherd to neighbors and friends, and he always had time to squat and talk with a passerby, either on his front porch or under the large apple trees in the front lawn. As kids we helped him farm, and often rode his horses or hunted rabbits, squirrels, and grouse in his fields.

Grandpa Jones brought a son, Forest, into his marriage with Mary. Dad remembers Forest as being a tremendous athlete, large, fast, and very muscular. He was also a troublemaker, and had a reputation as a hard drinker, fighter, and lover. He eventually killed a man in a fight over the man's wife, and died in prison at a young age.

Harry, Dad's beloved older brother, died a long, lingering death from tuberculosis. He was only in his early twenties, and Dad still grieves for him more than sixty-five years later.

The family thus included Bill Shouldis, Oakley Harper, Forest, Hattie, Harry, Opa, Lincoln, Francis, Raymond, and Curtis Jones. Bill died at age seventy-two, Oakley at fifty, Forest at thirty-five, Hattie at ninety, Harry at twenty-two, Lincoln at fifty-seven, Francis at eighty, and Raymond at sixty-two. Dad and Curtis live at this writing. Dad is ninety-two, and Curtis is seventy-eight, and both are doing well.

My father is a quiet, very capable man of great intelligence and abilities. Of medium size and greater than average strength, he spent over forty years working for DuPont in many positions. He can fix automobiles, wire and plumb a house, farm, and hunt and fish with the best of them. He is deeply religious, and is fully committed to living a Christian life.

While he was with DuPont, he mostly worked the swing shift, but always found time to attend football games and be active in boy scouts, PTA, and other civic groups. He's a very good and admirable man respected by all those who know him.

Dad and my mother, Mary, had three children. Glen was born in 1939, I was born in 1941, and Lenora five years later. Lenora developed diabetes at age twenty, and though she stayed healthy through most of her life, she died of stomach cancer at age fifty-seven. She was tall, dark, and beautiful, and studied art and taught for a short time. She also did some interior decorating. She had degrees from Cincinnati University and the University of Charleston. She was first married to James Faulkner, with whom she had a daughter, Anna. Jimmy died very young, and Lenora later married Mark Harris. She was married to Mark when she died.

Glen grew up an ideal oldest son. Respectful and ambitious, tall and handsome, intelligent and quiet, he was a source of pride for his parents. He participated in sports early on but lost interest in high school. Grades were no problem, and he graduated from West Virginia University in 1962 with a degree in mechanical engineering. He worked for several different companies in his career, including Westinghouse and Weyerhauser. He married Martha Vealie in 1964, and they have two sons, Jeffrey and Brian.

I was born in a small house along a busy highway north of Charleston on December 21, 1941. No hospital was needed as Mother was strong and I was her second child. My birthday came not long after Japan's raid on Pearl harbor, one of the most traumatic days in modern history.

My earliest memory is of the day five years later when Mother came home from the hospital with baby Lenora. I remember Lenora's first steps, and other vivid details from my childhood. I remember watching a log building burn, our basement flooding (many times, as the creek was just behind our house), sandlot football games, wrecks on the highway just in front of our house, playing Tarzan with good buddies, cutting brush on Dad's five acres, riding our horse, Princess, bareback, hoeing corn, boxing

From Dawn Until Dusk

with my brother Glen and my friends the Nestor boys and Rodney Jones, and picking tomatoes and berries. Being color blind, I wasn't able to tell red from green, and so wasn't a champion picker.

When I was about eleven I started thinking about girls and also about needing money. I was a big, strong kid but basically quite lazy, but I overcame that and began earning money when I could.

I started out mowing lawns for one dollar with a push mower, then worked at a greenhouse down the road, nailing together flats at six cents each. The greenhouse job lasted for a year or more until the day I got into a fight with a neighbor boy. In the melee we destroyed more boxes than I could build in a week.

At age eleven I left Buena Vista Grade School and went off to junior high in Sissonville.

For several years my greatest ambition had been to play football. So now in August I found myself finally putting on a helmet and pads. And while I spent most of that first year on the bench, I learned a great deal. For instance, I learned that pads and uniforms aren't made to fit little kids; big shoes rub blisters; and I learned something about human wickedness when Rodney Jones and I were attacked and beaten up by older hooligans at lunchtime between practices.

But the next year was different. Our uniforms fit better and we were part of a winning team. Football was my dream, and I was finally getting to play.

About this time I also started noticing a spicy little redhead singer named Eunice Holmes. Now I had two things on my mind: football and Euni. Academics hadn't arrived yet. Fortunately for me my grades came easy, and even though I made little effort my marks were mostly A's, even then.

August 1955 found me and my football buddies geared up and excited for the upcoming season. We had a great group of boys that had played together since grade school. Rodney and I were elected captains, and our first game was with last year's champions, Nitro. The game was close, and near the end we were in a position to push across the winning score. But our runner dropped the ball on their goal line, they recovered, and we lost by one point.

Coach Whittington was determined we would not lose again. We began scrimmaging with the high school junior varsity team. I made a difficult tackle on a husky runner, dislocated my shoulder, and broke my collarbone. When the doctor said I was done for the season, it also broke my heart. I watched my buddies win all their other games and then the championship without me.

Summers found me doing odd jobs but also spending a lot of time swimming and playing basketball. Most of the guys were jitterbugging with the pretty girls, but I was too timid for that. Though I didn't play much basketball in high school, I did participate in track—running long sprints and throwing the discus. Spring track at Sissonville was mostly used to stay in shape for football. Football was king at our school—all else was irrelevant.

In August of 1956 I started my sophomore year in high school with great expectations. I was fourteen but already stood six foot one and weighed 165 pounds. Coach Sawyers put me at offensive end, but also worked me at guard and tackle. For our first game with Saint Albans, coach played me a little at end. Our second game was against Nitro. They had a 235-pound, notoriously vicious, all-state tackle, and while our tackle was about the same size, he wasn't vicious at all. Early in the first quarter our gentle giant was knocked out cold and carried off the field. Coach looked around. And even though I tried to hide, he pointed at me. "Jones, go in for Eugene at tackle!" I grabbed my helmet and ran onto the field—scared nearly to tears.

When we lined up, the monster across from me growled, "You are dead meat, punk!" At the snap he whacked me across the helmet with his big hairy paw. I heard church bells. I went to the official and complained that the guy was playing dirty and trying to kill me. He was slugging, and this wasn't legal, at least I didn't think it was.

Next play he slugged me again, and while I tried to stop the chimes, the official ran up to him and yelled, "You, out of here!" I was saved! I went on to have a good game, and played regularly through the rest of our ho-hum season.

Everybody thought that the next year, 1957, was to be our year. Almost all our starters were returning, and we were optimistic, even a little cocky. Coach now had me at both offensive and

From Dawn Until Dusk

defensive guard—and promised me I would get a shot at fullback and linebacker. Guard was a good position for me as I now weighed about 185 pounds.

As always, our first game was at Saint Albans. They were a AAA powerhouse, and clearly headed to the state championship. We fielded twenty-seven players while they had almost one hundred. They also had an all-state guard and an all-state running back. But we played them to a 0-0 tie in 100 degree heat.

We won the next several games and then met AAA Dunbar. They fielded a future college division one quarterback, a tackle, and a wide receiver, and while they beat us twenty-four to twenty-one, they had negative yardage on the ground. Their four touchdown passes did us in.

We kept winning in our division until the last game against Poca High School. We were number one in AA and Poca was number two. They had a great team, with the state sprint champion at running back. We played to a thirteen-thirteen tie, which was enough to exclude us both from the AA playoffs.

By now I was getting a little more serious about both school and Euni. In my junior year I won the physics award, and was honored with an honorable mention all-state.

In the summer of 1958 I was working at a gas station owned by Euni's brothers, Orville and Darrell. In May, early in the morning after taking Euni home on prom night, I fell asleep at the wheel and rolled Dad's fifty-seven Chevy. I was very lucky not to have been hurt or killed.

At work during the summer, one of the regular loafers at the gas station, an avid football fan, took me aside and told me something I have never forgotten. He said, "You guys are going to have a great team, and you are going to make all state." Pretty heady stuff, especially since we had graduated almost everyone from the very good team of 1957, and Rodney and I were the only returning regulars.

I was now playing tackle, and at 190 pounds I was the biggest guy on the field. We would be starting at least five sophomores. Overall we averaged about 145 pounds, and our quarterback weighed only 120. We had no way of knowing it at the time, but three of the boys who were juniors on this team and two of the sophomores would be all-staters as seniors. One of the sophomores was destined to be an all-American linebacker at Marshall University, and have a great career in the pros.

Despite all this talent, our coach confided in me years later that he hadn't expected us to win a game. I'm sure glad he didn't tell us that at the time, because we were cocky enough to believe differently.

We lost three games in 1958, but they all were close games to AAA schools. We soon found ourselves in the championship game in our division. We lost to a very good Clarksburg team by six points in the rain and mud. We probably could have won in dry conditions, as they averaged over 200 pounds and thus had an advantage in the slop.

True to the gas station guy's prediction, we had a great season, and I made all-everything. I was first team all-state, first team all-southern (a greater honor because this included players from all-size schools), and later (one of only three athletes from West Virginia), honorable mention scholastic coaches all-American.

College letters came every day. They arrived from Florida, Colorado, Tennessee, Marshall, West Virginia University, Maryland, Rutgers, Virginia Tech, and others, all wanting me to come visit. Coaches started coming to our school and even met me at home.

A fantastic player from another team, Dave Santrock, and I had become friends; and we were both being recruited by the same schools. Together we visited Florida State, Maryland, Virginia Tech, and Marshall, but we both knew from the beginning that West Virginia University was the only place for us.

In May of 1959 I graduated third in a class of ninety-three. A B in typing was the blemish that kept me from the top, but I was the only boy in the top twenty.

After we committed to WVU, Coach "Pappy" Lewis found Dave and me summer jobs surveying on the new I-77 construction near Sissonville, one of the added benefits of a WVU football scholarship. This job suited us just fine, as we both planned to study engineering in school.

Euni and I had fallen quite in love. She was busy trying to finish school at Morris Harvey and working part time as well.

The summer ended too soon. August 1959 found me at Jackson's Mill in WVU football camp. We had daylight to dark

From Dawn Until Dusk

football practice as well as football classes. These guys were serious!

When I left home I was feeling pretty cocky. But when I arrived in Morgantown and saw the physiques, Hollywood good looks, and arrogant swaggers of my fellow players, I felt very small and out of place. When we began practice and I realized I was one of the smallest and slowest, I became even more intimidated. I was also the youngest at seventeen.

The coaches must have thought I was okay, however, as I became starting offensive guard and co-captain of our freshman team, along with Jim "Shorty" Moss.

Our freshman season wasn't great, and my first semester of classes was almost disastrous. High school had been too easy, and I had not had adequate courses to prepare me for the engineering program. The first term was spent playing football and staying up late over card games. The result was a C-minus average, with one F and one D. This scared me, so second semester I buckled down somewhat and improved to a B-minus average.

In the summer of 1960, Dave Santrock and I again worked construction, and then went back to football camp in August. We now had a new head coach, "Gentleman" Gene Corum, and because of my age and a glut of sophomore scholarship players, he decided to redshirt me, along with a dozen or so others.

Dave and I conferred during camp, and decided to room together in an apartment. Further discussion revealed he was changing his major from engineering to pre-med. After very little thought I decided to switch to pre-dental so we could have some of the same classes together. This flippant decision dramatically changed my life.

Even while this redshirt year cooled my interest in football, academics became increasingly important to me. I was the top student in all my chemistry, physics, anatomy, and math classes, and by the end of our two years together Dave and I had risen to the top of everything except French. My overall average was now 3.75 of a possible 4.0.

Euni and I were married on September 16, 1961, but Dave and I continued to room together while Euni finished school at Morris Harvey. I applied to dental school at WVU and was accepted to start in September, 1962. DuPont provided summer employment for sons of employees, so luck was with me again.

That fall of 1962 Euni and I found an apartment, and our life together began in earnest. She secured a teaching position at Brookhaven Elementary, and I soon found myself excelling at dentistry. I surged to the top of my class, and after the first semester received a tuition scholarship reserved for top students. I kept the scholarship for seven semesters.

After my third year I accepted a position with the United States Public Health Service, serving as a dentist in the federal prison at Danbury Connecticut. Euni was also employed for the summer with the fledgling Head Start program.

In May 1966 I graduated summa cum laude, with top awards in several specialty fields. I was offered first choice of any position with the USPHS division of Indian Health, and chose the Flathead Reservation in Northwest Montana.

Our first son, Mark, joined us February 8, 1966. In July Euni and I said goodbye to our folks, loaded little Mark and a few things into our 1964 Dodge Dart, and headed west.

We were stationed in the little town of Saint Ignatius, Montana, and lived next door to the Indian Health Station. I was close by when needed, and was always home for lunch. I hunted and fished when I could, and learned quite a lot caring for the Indian people; a very good preparation for my own practice to come later.

I thought I had found paradise in the beautiful Flathead Valley, and our little boy Mark was imprinted early with the love of wild places and beautiful country. Euni unfortunately never felt quite at ease there. She was isolated from family and friends, and I was often absent, gone into the mountains, hunting and trapping.

The two years of my assignment passed quickly, and we were soon back in West Virginia. I practiced dentistry near our home in Sissonville. My office was adjacent to the high school, and given the patronage of extended families and friends, I was immediately busy—and stayed that way for the next fifteen years.

Our second son, Allen, joined us in 1970, a beautiful blond boy with a bubbly personality. Shortly after his arrival we built our dream home on one hundred acres near my office on Martin's Branch Drive.

We had fourteen good years and a great life there, but western

From Dawn Until Dusk

vacations and memories kept drawing us back to Montana. For several years a small ranch west of Phillipsburg, Montana, had been our summer home. The boys loved to spend time shooting gophers and exploring through the mountains.

Later we bought a 959-acre farm in Ritchie County, West Virginia, and for a few years gave our energy and attention there. We sold our place in Montana but didn't forget the state.

In the fall of 1981 a call came from Dr. Ken Boom in Livingston, Montana. He was retiring, and had an office and practice to sell. He would accept the price of the real estate only.

Euni and I flew out to take a look. The deal seemed too good to be true, but we said we'd think about it. On the way home we decided to go for it. Why not?

I sold my practice and building to Greg Briscoe, my associate and brother-in-law, and in June of 1982, Euni, the boys, and I headed west to Montana again.

Since 1979, art and sculpture had played increasingly large roles in my life. The skills I had developed as a dentist led quite naturally into bronze sculpture. But I had found that bronze foundries and a market for sculpture were both more prevalent in the West than in West Virginia. By moving to Montana I hoped for a chance to develop a second career in bronze art.

Soon after settling in Livingston, we looked for an art gallery location, finding ten acres with a house along the road south to Yellowstone Park. We initially wanted to build only a small building to house our gallery, but our plans expanded until we soon had not only our gallery but a larger space next door rented as a sporting goods store. Shortly after we occupied this building, we built a wildlife museum as well.

We had accumulated many personal trophy mounts, and we bought and mounted others to complete our collection of North American wildlife. Eventually we had over one hundred life-sized animals, mounted primarily by me, with help from Mark and Allen when they had time.

Soon the museum was attracting visitors from all over, and was a draw for the other businesses as well. We moved our gallery to the original remodeled house and built a theatre building next door. Later we added a house behind our gallery, and sold the other lots and buildings, keeping only the gallery and the house.

In 1992 we decided to close the dental office, move to a ranch we had bought in 1990, and concentrate fully on my developing art career. Our gallery employee, Robin Berg, would be left in charge of running the gallery. Euni and I would concentrate on my sculpture and her pottery, do some shows, and enjoy life at the ranch.

We also decided to spend more time with our aging folks in West Virginia. Our sons were now in college and medical school. We built a small log home in West Virginia, and while we still spend April through November in Montana, December through March is spent in West Virginia.

We closed the gallery in 2004, but I continued to pursue my art. My career has flourished, and I now have over two hundred bronzes produced in limited editions. Euni is as active as ever in marketing.

Mark is a successful dermatologist in Billings, Montana, specializing in micro surgery of cancer on the face. He's married to Michaela, from Butte, Montana, and they have three beautiful girls—Morgan, Baylee, and Kasey.

Allen is a creative writer, and has published more than one hundred articles, essays, and short stories. He worked as editor of the magazine *Big Sky Journal* for five years after college, then gave this up to concentrate on his novel, *Last Year's River*, which was published through Houghton Mifflin. He is married to Karen Kenyon, from the San Francisco Bay area and New York.

The boys and I enjoy hunting and traveling to wild places around the world, but our ranch remains our favorite place to work and play. Euni and I also built a home near Billings and our three beautiful granddaughters. Luckily we were able to purchase acreage adjacent to Mark's, and in November of 2005 we moved in.

Most of my life has been a procession of fortunate successes born of determination, confidence, and much effort. Nothing has been easy, and nothing given. But by great good fortune I had wonderful, loving parents, and grew up in a time of security, harmony, and patriotism. I fell in love with a good and faithful woman, and have two great sons with whom to share my experiences and memories. They are my love and pride.

Part II

Chapter 1

Ol' Enik

In the Appalachia of my youth, hunting was considered an honorable pastime. Skins were sold for valued pennies and the meat was always a welcome addition to the table. An accurate gun was as important as a plow, and a good hunting dog was worth its weight in gold. Nearly every family had a "coon" or "possum" dog that was also used for squirrels, rabbits, and birds. They were beagles or beagle crosses, for the most part. The farmers and their kids were fiercely proud of their dogs, and many yarns were swapped concerning the prowess of this or that nondescript mutt. The days of specialization were still far in the future; dogs were meant to be hunting dogs, not just bird dogs or rabbit dogs or treeing dogs. They were expected to do it all.

Ol' Enik was the best of a great breed. Muscular but thin, with bony legs and big feet, his coat was black and short, graying as he aged. Both ears stood upright when he was a pup but the tips folded over as he matured. A true intelligence shone from his dark eyes—and not just a little mischief.

Enik belonged to my Grandpa Jones, and was a one-family dog. He was so smart he learned to distinguish the sounds of different approaching vehicles. My grandparents lived up a one-

From Dawn Until Dusk

lane dirt road on a seventy-acre hill farm. Like most dogs in the area, Enik lived under the porch, sleeping and snapping at flies and yellow jackets. There were enough people in the valley to provide a considerable amount of vehicle traffic on the road, but if any of Enik's hunting buddies came to visit, Grandma would know long before they were within sight of the house because Enik would suddenly become alert, bolt out from under the porch, and dash down the road in a cloud of dust.

If you had ever been hunting with Enik, you would be greeted by him a mile or more from the house. He would joyously jump and run around your car, grinning and slobbering and wagging all over himself in his joy. If it was hunting season, he would greet you with even greater enthusiasm. And when the guns were uncased he literally exploded with joy. But for those neighbors who didn't hunt, Enik wouldn't even open his eyes or lift his ears.

In the field, Enik was a gifted mind reader. If the game of the day was squirrels, Enik knew immediately, and set about trailing and treeing the gray and fox squirrels bouncing through the undergrowth and canopies of oak and hickory. He would trail silently, barking only when a squirrel was sighted and treed. He never seemed to fail.

He was equally adept at trailing and treeing animals at night, and many a possum or coon was bagged to the tune of his deep baritone bark. At the end of the trail, this bark took on a different, quite distinctive, treeing tone.

As great as he was as a treeing dog, Enik shone best in the pursuit of his favorite quarry, cottontail rabbits. To rabbit hunt in those days, the hunters would form a skirmish line some thirty to fifty feet apart, kicking through the bush as they walked, hoping to flush rabbits from their daytime beds and shoot them with scatterguns as they scurried away through the weeds.

The duty of the hounds was to help jump the rabbits and, if they weren't shot on the jump, to then trail them and bring them around in a circle for another try. Most fields were dotted with brush piles as farmers fought to keep the hillsides clear, stacking brush as they cut it. Cottontails liked to hide in these piles, often feeling so secure that they had to be literally kicked from their beds. Enik knew this as well as any veteran hunter. He would circle a brush pile and, if his nose told him a rabbit was hidden in there, would look back at the hunters to make sure they were ready. He would then plunge into the brush, flushing the rabbit. In some cases, he would jump on the pile and bounce on it like a trampoline until the rabbit squirted out. He loved the game and played his part to perfection.

In those days, when most farmers raised some grain (and their harvesting of it was primitive and inefficient) there were many bobwhite quail in the fields and fencerows. These birds were a welcome addition to our rabbit hunts. Though Enik made no classic point, if he winded birds he would pause in midstride. The quail would usually hold well, and Enik would restrain himself until the hunter approached. He would then leap in amongst them and jump around like crazy as they flushed.

One day, toward the end of a hunt, we approached an old overgrown plum orchard thick with weeds and briars. As the visibility was poor, ol' Enik soon disappeared from sight. We yelled back and forth trying to locate him, but he was apparently solid on point inside the thicket. We began to push our way into the tangle. Suddenly the air was full of quail, flushing in every direction. And Enik was right behind them, sailing up over the thicket as if shot from a gun.

Gaping in surprise, we watched as, at least eight feet off the ground, he caught the last bird in his mouth. He dropped back into the brush and swallowed the bird whole. He came out with a proud grin and feathers stuck to his lips. This was the only time he ever ate a game bird or animal. I suppose he felt he deserved that one.

On another occasion Dad, brother Glen, and I had been hunting rabbits before noon on a warm and drizzly day. We'd had a good hunt and, with help from Enik, had bagged several cottontails. As we passed on the hillside above a neighbor's barnyard, we were joined by his beautiful purebred beagle. This dog was a quite famous rabbit chaser and we weren't unhappy to welcome him to our hunt. Enik immediately began to show signs of jealousy, sulking as the beagle began to chase his rabbits. Enik would not hunt the rest of the day but moped and trailed at our heels all afternoon. The beagle performed admirably and we praised him well as we dropped him off on our way home. Enik followed us home and crept under the porch with not a wag.

From Dawn Until Dusk

Later that evening we noticed he was gone from under the porch. Just as we began to worry, ol' Enik came swinging up the muddy road with a big, smug grin and wagging tail. We were relieved he was back to his old self.

As we drove down the road toward home, however, we were stopped by the neighbor who owned the beagle. He was fuming. It seems ol' Enik had decided his honor had been injured. He had come into the neighbor's barnyard and thrashed the daylights out of that beagle.

Ol' Enik lived to a ripe old age, becoming an even better rabbit dog as the years slowed him a little. When he finally lay down for good, he was missed by us all—especially when we came to visit and he was not there to welcome us home.

Chapter 2

West Virginia Deer Hunting

Sometimes a big game trophy can be dangerous even after it's down. The last kick of a dying animal or a heart attack while you're packing it out can add an unpredictable element of risk to the hunt.

When my dad was still a young man and I was just out of dental school, we arranged with some friends to set up a deer camp in the mountains of eastern West Virginia. A deer camp in West Virginia was a cherished tradition, and ours consisted of a twelve-by-fourteen foot wall tent just off a logging road at the top of "Molly's Hill."

The area was a mixture of hardwood forest, laurel thickets, and rugged cliffs. The woods teemed with whitetail deer and turkeys, but good bucks were hard to find. With pressure heaviest along the roads, a hunter's only chance for a mature buck was to hike back away from any motorized access. This was long before ATVs ruined traditional hunting. The backcountry went untouched except by a hardy few.

Dad was a determined and usually successful hunter who spent long hours in the woods pursuing the wily old mossy horns.

From Dawn Until Dusk

Burl's father, Opa, right, and Uncle Bob Bumgardner took these two West Virginia does in 1965.

His strategy was to leave camp long before first light and, with a flashlight, trek several miles into the forest. He would then select a stand overlooking a likely area and quietly watch and listen until sunrise. Sometimes a buck sneaking back to his bed would fall to this tactic, but more often Dad would leave his stand to begin a long day of creeping silently through the thickets.

Still hunting was his specialty, and he would often surprise bucks while they were in their beds, shooting them before they knew he was anywhere in the vicinity. Then began the very arduous task of dragging the buck up and over the mountain to camp. Often by the time a trophy reached camp it hardly looked like a deer at all, with the hair scraped from his sides and the carcass frozen stiff as a board.

One morning was like most all mornings on Molly's Hill. Dad left early and hiked south over a low ridge toward the mountain beyond. I went in the opposite direction, across the road and down into an old clear-cut that had grown back in with brush eight-to-ten feet tall. The evening before I had discovered an old abandoned tree stand in a large black oak that overlooked the clear-cut. Now, and with much difficulty, I located the tree stand in the dark and carefully climbed the fifteen feet up into the seat. It seemed sturdy enough, so I relaxed to wait for shooting light.

It was a cold morning, and I was soon chilled to the bone, shivering violently. I worried that I wouldn't be able to shoot even if a buck did come along. With first light the forest came alive with sound. Gray squirrels chattered through wet branches, moving into the hickories to feed. Chipmunks played in the leaves. Soon I heard another sound. At first I thought a deer was approaching, but then I could see the orange caps of two hunters working their way toward me. Disappointed at the intrusion, I watched them sit on a log just a stone's throw around the hill, unaware of my presence.

Even though I knew my chances were diminished, I decided to make the best of the situation and stay put for a while. The next hour was spent watching squirrels and inspecting every new and suspicious sound on the forest floor. The cold was almost unbearable. My friends below were beginning to fidget and whisper to each other.

Every few seconds I would scan the openings and trails below, but I detected no movement at all. Eventually, as the morning brightened, I heard strange noises from down the valley. At first it sounded like dogs barking, but then I could distinguish the voices of men yelling and whooping. It was a deer drive, and it further disturbed my plan for the morning.

Just as I decided to give up, I spotted movement near the far edge of the clear-cut at least three hundred yards away. Through my scope, I saw a pair of white antlers moving through the low brush. The antlers looked big, and my heart began to pound. Between the cold and the excitement, I was soon trembling so uncontrollably I thought I might fall from my perch.

Forcing myself to settle down I peered again at an opening just ahead of where I had seen the buck. Within seconds the antlers appeared again—followed shortly by a neck and body as the buck snuck down the narrow trail. It was now or never. As the crosshairs found their mark, my rifle boomed across the valley.

The hunters below jumped up, stared at me in disbelief, and moved off, cussing. I glanced back to where the buck had been but could see no sign of him. Gathering my belongings and unloading my rifle, I shimmied down the tree to the forest floor. With relief I

From Dawn Until Dusk

slapped my sides and jumped around to renew the circulation in my frozen hands and feet.

Taking a bearing on a white snag near where the buck had been, I quickly walked through the noisy leaves and across the little basin to the far side. The buck was nowhere to be seen. I circled the area with growing fear that I had missed him—then I saw a white antler sticking out of the ground tangle. I had him, and he was a beauty.

As I began to field dress him and contemplate the relatively short drag, I heard someone moving toward me. It was Dad. "I heard that big rifle boom and I knew it had to be you," he said. "And I knew there would be fresh liver tonight."

Dad had changed his mind about where to hunt that morning and had instead taken a stand near an old tree he remembered—just a half mile or so from where I was. A lucky break for me because I now had help with the one job we always dreaded: the drag back to camp. We were less than a mile away, however, so we had the buck hung beside our tent before anyone else was back for lunch. As this was opening day of season, Dad decided to go back out and try again.

As the guys came in, my story was told over and over again. They couldn't believe my luck, especially since I insisted it was pure skill. I even volunteered to shoot their bucks for them. I never told them that I had the guys on the deer drive to thank for my good fortune.

After lunch they all returned to the woods with visions of monster bucks of their own. I stayed in camp to prepare a whatchyagot stew deluxe.

About an hour before sunset I heard some shooting down the ridge from camp and a single shot from across the ridge on the mountain. As shadows darkened the hollows, the guys straggled back into camp with their own stories. Over steaming plates of stew, they shared the adventures of the day. Everyone had seen bucks, and our friend Judd had missed a spike just above camp. Another friend, Ron, had taken a stand before daybreak. At first light a big gobbler flushed from the tree just a few feet above his head, giving him a terrible start. Deer had paraded around him all day but there were no bucks.

As we washed the dishes, I thought about Dad. It was common

for him to stay out long past dark, but I always worried about him. He knew no fear, and might wander for miles during a normal day's hunt. Three hours after sunset we decided to go look for him. We started by cruising the roads in our pickup, hoping to find him on his way back to camp.

When he left he had started off to the east, down the ridge behind camp. We drove off in the same direction, and had only traveled a couple miles when I spotted Dad trudging along in the headlights, obviously exhausted.

Back in camp with a steaming bowl of stew and a peanut butter sandwich, he rehashed his adventure of the afternoon.

After leaving camp he had crossed the ridge and decided to hunt along the top of a cliff on the other side. Around 4:30 he approached an immense laurel thicket below the cliff face. There were numerous small ledges on the cliff, making it a perfect hiding place for a buck. He slowed to a snail's pace and scanned every possible spot ahead. Soon he spotted an antler and a foreleg behind a scrubby white oak about halfway up the face of the cliff. As he maneuvered around above the buck, he began to see more of him. From a distance of less than fifty yards he shot him in his bed. The animal died instantly.

The buck was especially interesting as he had survived being shot in the left shoulder years before and had a crippled leg as a result. Because of this injury his antlers had become gnarled and deformed—and he obviously had become very wary. He was a great trophy!

The day was still young but Dad recognized he had a problem. The cliff extended for miles. If he went down, it would mean a long, long drag around and back to camp. He felt he had to bring the buck up the cliff and over the ridge. By tying the deer to the tree he was able to field dress it, but when he tried to pull it up the cliff he couldn't budge it. Having plenty of rope he devised a crude pulley system that allowed him to move the buck, inch by inch, up the cliff. Not wanting to leave the animal to the scavengers, he had struggled until long after dark before finally leaving it hanging in a tree.

"Want to go back and get him tonight?"

He looked at me first in disbelief, but after a few minutes of rest, said, "Why not?"

From Dawn Until Dusk

So Ron, Judd, Dad and I headed back up the ridge at 11:00 with flashlights and lots of joking and laughter. Dad, with his unerring woodsmanship, led us directly to the buck. With the added manpower, we quickly maneuvered the animal up the cliff and down the mountain to the road.

At the end of the week the other guys still had not connected, but everyone had a great time and we parted with plans to meet again. Dad had impressed all once again with his skills and hard work, and everyone took a little of the venison home.

Chapter 3

Persistence

Many years after my boyhood experiences hunting rabbits and squirrels on my grandparents' farms, I was able to buy some farm property of my own, over three hundred acres on Higgenbottom Creek, part of the same valley in which Dad had grown up. The ground was long neglected, and had reverted to mixed hardwood timber with brushy fields and overgrown apple, plum, and peach orchards. The buildings were crumbled and rotted—the last remnants of the families that had once called them home.

Dad was often saddened to return to Higgenbottom. When he lived there as a boy the families were young and active and the farms were clean and well kept. Now only the ghosts of memory kept vigil there.

Though it was a place of nostalgia for me as well, my memories were much more recent and pleasant, and the land was now perfect deer and turkey habitat. When Dad had lived there, horses were the mode of transportation, the hillsides were clean, and the very rare appearance of a deer was the topic of conversation for weeks. Now deer were much more common (though still not

From Dawn Until Dusk

numerous) and really big bucks were occasionally taken. This is a story about one hunt for a Higgenbottom buck.

Persistence is essential to hunting as it is in most endeavors of life. It is not only required to find a trophy but even more important in trailing and retrieving a wounded animal. In this hunt persistence finally paid off.

I slipped through the apple trees of the abandoned orchard in Higgenbottom Creek on a frosty morning. The sun was still hidden from the valley floor and misty fog filled the overgrown field. Apples littered the grass under the trees. The morning promised to be ideal as the heavy frost revealed the tracks of several deer in the flattened grass under the trees. Soon I spotted what I hoped to find: a large fresh scrape with a huge track right in the center.

Past the orchard was a confusion of grapevine and greenbrier thickets. The deer were somewhere up ahead in the tangle. I knew from previous hunts that an approach from my current position would only push the deer out ahead of me. I just needed to figure out how to find them before they realized I was in there with them. To make matters worse, even though it was now perfectly calm, thermal currents would soon carry my scent ahead. I needed to get out of the valley before sunrise started the air moving.

The hillsides were steep but not high. Before long I had vacated the bottoms and was above the fog on the ridge north of Higgenbottom Creek. My plan was to now still hunt as slowly and quietly as possible around the ridges two to three miles east, working my way to the head of the valley. The half circle was accomplished in a couple hours, and luckily no deer were spooked out ahead of me. Frost still glittered in the sunrise as I began my descent into the valley—now from the opposite direction and into the gathering breeze.

The buck was in there—I knew he was! The problem was how to find him and get a shot before he vanished into the dense cover. Conditions were perfect: sun to my back, wind in my face, and wet leaves underfoot. I moved a step and paused, moved a step and paused, my eyes darting back and forth, trying to penetrate the dense cover.

Suddenly a doe exploded from the brush just ahead. After only a few hops she stopped and looked back. I thought she had seen me but she was looking back at . . . what? My eyes burned as I struggled to see through the dense thickets. And then suddenly there he was: A magnificent frozen statue in a frosty halo of scrub pine and grapevine.

His antlers looked huge, but I couldn't stop to admire him. With mature bucks like this one, a long second was more than one usually had before they were gone. As he stared toward the doe my rifle came up—and the shot echoed through the huge oaks. The range was fifty feet or less, and my grip on my rifle was solid, with no tremors. The buck erupted, bounding immediately out of sight. As he crashed through the heavy brush, it sounded like he fell into the deep hollow below.

I couldn't believe he hadn't dropped in his tracks. I lowered the gun, levered in another cartridge, and slipped over to where he had been standing. I began to doubt the event was real. I couldn't have missed at that range. Then I saw the blood . . . lots of blood. I followed the trail for a few steps, and then heard branches crash ahead of me. I glimpsed the buck as he went up the next little ridge and then seemed to fall again. My spirits soared. I thought he was down for good. But when I ran up to where he had fallen he had again disappeared.

Resigned to a long trailing job, I concentrated on the tracks in the damp soil (I have a red and green color weakness, which makes it very difficult for me to follow a blood trail). He led me up and over the next big ridge before I lost all sign of him. I circled and searched the rest of the day until darkness forced me to give it up.

Tired and discouraged, I drove home. I got on the phone with my old friend Raymond and told him about my problem, about the great buck lying dead up there somewhere. As I knew he would, he volunteered to go back with me next morning—and I knew he was a great tracker.

Daylight found Ray and me at the head of Higgenbottom Creek. I led him to where I had shot the buck and he immediately took up the trail. Ray was able to follow the buck for an additional mile or more, one drop at a time. The buck seemed to be circling back before we again lost the trail and were forced to give up. The rest of the day was spent looking in likely spots and combing

From Dawn Until Dusk

the area as thoroughly as possible, to no avail. And then it started to rain.

As much as I hated to do it, common sense told me to give it up. Rain fell steadily the next day. And while I didn't even go out of the house, I couldn't forget that great buck.

Next day was Saturday and Dad was off work. I had told him about the buck and where I had decided he must be. I imagined he'd been circling back into the thickets where I had first seen him—probably his secure bedding area.

Dad agreed to go back once again even though it was still raining and had been for a day and half. We again went to the head of the hollow and retraced the trail Ray and I had followed. We then split up to comb the thickets back down the hollow toward the truck. By noon we were drenched and thoroughly dejected, with still no sign of the buck.

After a soggy lunch we decided to call it quits, but thought we should make one last sweep of the pine jungle along the creek on our way out. We had gone only a few hundred feet when I heard Dad yell from across the draw.

I called back, "What did you say?"

"I think I found something you are looking for."

I hustled across toward his voice. After several minutes of struggling through dripping thickets, I finally saw Dad leaning over my buck. The animal lay there in the pine needles as if he were only asleep. The other beds around him confirmed that this had been his bedroom after all.

Good old Dad and persistence had paid off once again. Inspection of the carcass revealed that I had shot one inch lower than intended and had taken out the sternum and some lower ribs, but had not penetrated the heart or lungs. Bleeding had eventually taken its toll, and this hardy animal had returned to his lair to die.

Chapter 4

Mother Nature's Child

It was the summer of 1966 and I was fresh out of dental school, a new officer with the United States Public Health Service, Division of Indian Health. At my request I had been stationed on the Flathead Indian Reservation in Saint Ignatius, Montana. I'd never been to Montana, and had little idea of what to expect once I got there. As a fledgling hunter and fisherman, though, I had always been enamored with the romance and possibilities of the Rockies.

With my wife, Euni, and our six-month-old son, Mark (and a very big lump in my throat), we drove our 1964 Dodge Dart over a hill on Highway 93. The small town of Saint Ignatius appeared below us. And behind it? Ten thousand feet of waterfalls, pine forests, summer snowdrifts, and granite avalanche chutes. We were overwhelmed. We had discovered paradise.

My assignment was to provide dental care to some 2,500 tribal members in a public health facility. We found the folks friendly and open as we hung out our figurative shingle. Hearing about their way of life and their history excited and intrigued me. They did not seem to mind sharing their heritage with us and we were grateful to be accepted and appreciated.

From Dawn Until Dusk

Historically the Flathead had inhabited the Bitterroot valley to the south but had been displaced to the Mission valley. I learned about their chiefs and medicine men, their traditions and taboos, sweat houses and powwows, stick games and war dances—and about hunting and trapping on their land. I listened to stories of gigantic moose and elk, and the trophies left in the woods "because you can't eat antlers, even in soup." I heard about Chief Charlo, Louie Ninepipe and his songs, about the French influence in the area and of heroes past and present. Most information was provided by my dental assistant Charlene and her husband Clifford. They helped us in many ways to adapt to our new situation. I also heard about a man named Joe Wheeler.

Joe was born and spent most of his life on or near the Flathead Indian Reservation. Though he had white men among his ancestors, his coal black eyes, his dark skin, and his bearing were all very native. He married young and, when I knew him, he had one son and several daughters. A stern disciplinarian, he was loved and respected by his family. He had built a cozy house with corrals and barn on the North Fork of the Jocko, just on the edge of a vast wilderness. He had beaver ponds filled with lunker trout out his back door, as well as elk, deer, black and grizzly bears, mountain goats, and cougars. Marauding bears made tending livestock difficult so Joe kept horses and little else. The Jocko itself teemed with cutthroat and Dolly Varden, suckers, and whitefish. Joe was a great fisherman, but was usually interested in subsistence rather than sport. Rod, gig, or seine, he could lay up many pounds of fish in a single night, especially when Dolly Varden were spawning. His nearest neighbors were miles away, and in the winter he and his family were almost entirely isolated. He was as much a child of the wilderness as it was possible to be in the twentieth century.

Self-sufficiency and independence were as natural as breathing to Joe. He often talked about the time he left home after a spat with his folks and went into the mountains to live off the land. The story wasn't surprising until he added that he was only ten years old at the time.

As a teen and young adult, Joe was regarded as a little odd.

Joe Wheeler, his son, Joey, and a black bear trapped in the Missions, circa 1967.

Uneducated but very intelligent (with a particular interest in geology), he read extensively and audited college courses to learn about the mountains around him. He was also feared, a man to be avoided in a fight if at all possible. He bore the marks of many battles and accidents. His belly carried an immense ragged scar—the result of a chainsaw fight he had obviously lost. He often vomited bile from the internal damage of that fight. There were many stronger and larger men in the Flathead Valley that would give up the sidewalk to the dark and fiery little man with the wide smile and cold eye.

Having heard about Joe from so many admirers, I became determined to meet him. One day I drove up to introduce myself.

Stepping out of my truck in his yard, I was met with warmth

From Dawn Until Dusk

and good humor. Turns out, just a few hours before Joe had shot a marauding grizzly in his pig pen. He and his son Joey had received two pigs in a trade. They had put them in a pen and were feeding them in preparation for butchering in the late fall. An old boar grizzly passing through had scented the irresistible porkers and decided to make a meal of them, breaking through the pole corral and killing both pigs immediately. The commotion awakened the family but the bear had disappeared with one of the pigs before Joe could get into action with his old .300 Savage. Come sunrise Joe was out repairing the pen and preparing a reception should the griz return for the other pig. Joe left a three-foot opening on one side and placed the dead pig just inside, with an ancient steel bear trap concealed in the dirt in front of it.

About two o'clock the next morning they were all again awakened, this time by the sound of crashing timbers and roars of rage as the bear fought to escape the trap. Joe ran barefoot out into the frosty night and shot the furious bear. As the bear died, the valley again became silent and Joe and his family went back to bed until morning.

At sunrise Joe studied the beautiful animal lying in the remains of his corral. They weren't going to have pork but they weren't too disappointed that they now had a bear. He was quite large and very fat, with a silver-tipped black coat, thick and silky.

As Joe told the story in his good-humored, matter-of-fact way, I saw that he was indeed an unusual man. Someone from whom I could learn a great deal. We eventually became great friends and spent many days together. Though I was a greenhorn and novice compared to him, I felt that Joe could sense a commonality of spirit. He opened up to me as he had rarely done with others. We shared countless hours on the trails and beside campfires, hunting his wilderness playground together.

As I was so impressed and excited by his grizzly story, Joe volunteered to show me how to trap a bear out in the woods. Of course I couldn't wait to get started.

The north fork of the Jocko is home to a healthy population of bears—both griz and black. The upper reaches of Skunk Meadows were especially popular with the animals, and it was here that Joe chose to educate me on the finer points of trapping bears.

First we needed to build a box of sturdy poles. The dimensions would finally measure about six feet long by four feet high and two-and-a-half feet wide. While we talked, sawed, and hammered, Joe sang and told tall tales that kept his kids and me laughing. He was a gifted entertainer and had unlimited stories and songs.

That evening when our construction project was complete, Joe and I drove his old pickup, his German shepherd Shadow in the back, up into the mountains. We were looking for an elk or deer for his freezer—and offal he could use for bear bait. We hadn't gone far when Joe stopped and pointed across a ravine to a fat young mule deer buck feeding in heavy timber. I was amazed at his ability to see the deer so far away. It seemed too far to shoot but he quickly aimed and fired his iron-sighted .300 Savage, dropping the buck with a broken neck. Grunting, we wrestled the buck back to the truck. In the frosty evening we dressed and skinned the carcass and hung it to chill in his barnyard.

After hanging the meat Joe insisted I come to the house for a snack and more conversation. I really should have gone on home (I knew Euni would be worried about me) but I couldn't resist his magnetic personality and the promise of more adventure. Unfortunately the Wheelers were far from phone service—a call was impossible.

As we sat and talked, Joe opened up more and more, telling me about his secret places and hunting tactics; how he could call bull elk with just his tongue and a length of plastic pipe, and moose with just his voice. He'd shot a number of gigantic bulls over the years. Soon he had me so excited I couldn't wait for hunting season to open.

About ten o'clock Joe said, "Come with me tonight and I'll show you some game." I thought he was pulling my leg but he explained that he had packed over two hundred pounds of salt back on the mountain a few weeks earlier and he was sure we could find some elk there tonight. He needed some elk meat "real bad." We went back out to his corral where Joe saddled up his horse Buck and a white mare for me. We loaded them in the truck and headed off up into the mountain—giggling like two dumb kids.

From Dawn Until Dusk

After bouncing over boulders and ruts for what seemed like twenty miles Joe pulled off the road and into the trees. The horses were unloaded without a light as Joe didn't want to spook any animals that might be above us. He whispered, "Follow me." And mounted up. Once on my own horse, it was so dark I could not even see the mare's white ears. I could hear Joe's horse moving off and up through the trees, though, so I kicked the mare and let her follow on her own.

The darkness was so complete I lost all orientation. My horse tried her best to scrape me off on the trees we passed but I hung on with a death grip, cussing her quietly.

I'd grown up with horses, but had not sat a saddle for at least ten years. Yet here I was floating up a very steep mountainside behind a crazy man that could see in the dark, on a white horse that obviously would rather be without the two-hundred pounds of dude on her back. Eventually, after an eternity of this torture, I heard Joe stop and dismount. I was afraid to get off because on this steep mountainside it might be one-hundred feet or more to the first step. He quietly came back and told me to get off and we would walk the rest of the way. I now felt sure he was insane, but since I didn't know which way to run to get off the mountain, I stumbled along behind him.

A couple hundred steps uphill Joe stopped again. In a whisper he told me that across the ravine in front of us was a large meadow where he had placed the salt. We would sit on this big log until we heard elk.

I must say that at this point I was very impressed—what this Indian had already accomplished would have seemed impossible if I had not been there. I was still totally blind.

Joe had a light he planned to shine on the elk once we heard them. He would shoot from behind the light. If this sounds unsportsmanlike—well, you just needed to be there!

As we sat in the dark and I began to calm down, it didn't seem quite so crazy after all—darned if it wasn't kind of pleasant. Just as I began to really enjoy being there on that log, I heard brush crack down the slope below us.

"Is that an elk?" I whispered.

"Porcupine."

"Sounds bigger than a porcupine to me."

The cracking moved up toward us, accompanied by some low snuffling and rumbling.

"Sounds like a bear," I whispered.

"Just a porcupine."

The log we were on was a very long one, and was supported by downed timber below it. The noise moved diagonally up beside us and was getting quite close. I wondered if I might be eaten by a bear before I had a chance to trap one.

By this time I had the flashlight from Joe. When the log started to move under us I could stand it no longer. Trembling, I switched on the light and shone it down the log.

The porcupine was in fact the biggest, shiniest, scariest, closest black bear I had ever seen. Before my heart could get restarted, he was gone—head over heels down through that God-awful tangle of brush and briars.

Joe laughed until I thought he would fall off the mountain. Before long I was laughing with him. Two crazy fools on a mountainside in the middle of the night—with a bear!

I kept the light on all the way back down the mountain. Its pale beam revealed a series of hairpin switchbacks, narrow ledges, and dizzying drop offs. Joe's horses earned my respect that night and I trusted them with my life many times after that.

Joe thought the entire adventure was a great joke, and laughed over and over as we rode off the mountain. Of course I laughed too, even though I was the object of the joke.

As the sun was now beginning to light the east we decided to load up our box and the deer offal and drive up into Skunk Meadow to set our trap. By this time I was so caught up with the excitement and adventure I wasn't even thinking of Euni and the trouble I faced at home.

We chose a quiet glade criss-crossed with bear trails. After unloading the box and filling the back of it with deer intestines, we carefully set and concealed the steel trap in the mouth of the box, covering it with grass and leaves. The chain was wrapped and bolted around a large tree. After a final inspection of our set, we backed away and left with the sense of expectation that only trappers know.

From Dawn Until Dusk

By now it was afternoon. Driving back into town, I was apprehensive. Euni was going to kill me—and I deserved it! She stood in the door, waiting. But she surprised me with a big hug and said she was grateful I was still alive. She'd been all set to call for help if I wasn't home by dark. Lucky for me I had a sensible and forgiving wife.

For the next several days I drove up the Jocko after work to check the bear trap. Each day the trap was undisturbed. On the seventh day, a big black was waiting patiently for us at the end of the chain. He had demolished the cubby, torn up saplings and turf, and peeled all the bark from the big pine tree as far as the chain would let him reach. When we approached him it was obvious he was plain tuckered out. He ignored us with no offer to fight. Joey dispatched him cleanly with one shot from his little .22 rifle.

After trucking the bear back to his cabin, Joe revealed his Indian superstition regarding bears. He told me the Indians associated many human characteristics with bears and therefore chose to leave them alone—only skinning or handling them after dire necessity, or if they had been killed in self defense. He suggested I take the bear; he would rather not skin or butcher it because of the taboos. Later, as I came to know him better, I suspected he pulled my leg just a little.

I was delighted to have the bear, however, and was surprised at my good fortune—but after dozens of hours working and tanning the skin I began to suspect Joe had other motives for giving me the bear. He was probably still chuckling over another joke on me.

Joe and I made several trips into the mountains with his horses and spent many memorable hours riding the craggy ridges and climbing the towering peaks. Being a natural clown Joe kept me entertained with ribald songs and stories—while he educated me about hunting elk.

When the statewide hunting season finally arrived, Joe accompanied me into the remote areas surrounding the reservation. We often trekked into the back country at night to call and listen—locating bulls that were too shy or too wise to call in daytime. Sometimes the bulls would approach us in the dark and thrill us with their grunts, brays, and shrieks. Joe could imitate their sounds perfectly and they would soon be in a fighting frenzy—only to be disappointed as we slipped off into the dark. Eventually, with Joe's help, I managed to bag a bull of my own.

In addition to his horses, Joe had a dog, a huge German shepherd named Shadow. Dedicated and loving, Shadow would have died for Joe, and tried to please him in everything he did. Shadow was our companion as we packed and camped in the mountains and our bodyguard as we slept under the stars. Best of all Shadow was a blood tracker and recovery dog.

Shadow remained at Joe's side at all times. Even when game was in sight and he trembled with excitement he would not leave without a command. In the event an animal was wounded, which seldom happened, Joe would release Shadow. With a silent bound the dog would be after it. Usually he would lead us to a dead animal, but if it still lived Shadow would pull it down and finish it. Because of Shadow, Joe seldom, if ever, lost an animal.

Joe's horses were also well trained, but the white mare was slow and lazy. I think she didn't like me because I was heavier than what she was used to. On our pack trips we carried our bedroll and supplies behind the saddles, making for heavy loads. The trails we traveled were mostly animal paths, rough and very steep—sometimes very steep for miles.

On one climb, the mare stopped and with a huge sigh refused to go any further. I wanted to give her a rest but Joe insisted I break a switch and force her on. After a few licks she grudgingly continued to climb. Soon she stopped again, puffing like a locomotive. While I sat on her back, astonished, she swayed, and then fell right over on her side. I jumped free and yelled ahead to Joe that she was dead. But Joe knew better, and proceeded to jerk, beat, and cuss her until she jumped up, shook herself, and acted like nothing had happened. I think she was more afraid of him than of dying.

When I remounted she continued up the mountain with nary a complaint. From that moment I never questioned Joe's judgment concerning his animals.

His estimation of my abilities proved to be not as good. On one occasion he insisted I use his horses to take a dental school friend hunting in the mountains. He let me ride his horse Buck,

From Dawn Until Dusk

but asked that I take good care of him. He insisted I use a full-length red blanket under the saddle as Buck was the same color as a bull elk.

Buck was a great horse, and we spent several splendid days together with only one near catastrophe. While climbing a steep narrow trail across a shale slide that ended in a vertical drop, we came to a large flat rock on the trail. It was too wide for Buck to step across, and he refused to step directly on it. I thought he was being lazy, and remembering Joe's advice with the mare I stupidly broke a switch and forced him on. As soon as Buck's feet stepped on the rock, he slipped and fell over the side. Luckily I was able to hold onto the reins as I scrambled off on the uphill side. As we plummeted toward the precipice, I dug in and pulled on the reins with all my strength—finally getting the horse's head around. Scrambling, he was able to get his feet under him. We struggled back up to the trail as my friend stared bug-eyed.

Needless to say I had learned another valuable lesson. Even Joe's horse was smarter than me when it came to surviving in the mountains. Of course I never told Joe.

My stay with the Flatheads and my association with my Indian friends ended too soon. After two years I left them and returned to a dental practice in West Virginia.

A few years later Joe realized an ambition and began working in a gold mine. Disaster struck, however, and he died in the mine from poisonous gas.

His son, Joey, honored his father by placing Joe's body on Gray Wolf peak in his beloved Mission Mountain wilderness. Joe was a lucky man—he lived a life of which the rest of us can only dream.

Chapter 5

Goat Cliffs

I'd heard through the Flathead Valley grapevine that if you wanted to hunt mountain goats, eighteen-year-old Tom Mitchell was the expert. Tom came to the office as a dental patient and we soon became fast friends. Almost immediately we made plans for my first trip into the peaks of the Mission mountains.

Climbing around on the cliffs above timberline is not for the faint of heart. Winds strong enough to toss pebbles and precipices hundreds of feet deep stand in contrast to alpine lakes of emerald blue and meadows of green and gold, long barren ridges of stone and twisted snags of mountain juniper. Though summer is short in the high country, a fantastic number of plants and animals thrive there, from little whistling picas to giant grizzly bears. The most visible of these animals is the Rocky Mountain goat.

Goats live year round in the high country, protected by their long fleecy coats from winter's frigid blasts. Grazing on windswept ridges, the goats only descend in early spring as the grass emerges on the southern slopes. Except for this short period, goats live high above the usual threats, with only lions and eagles to fear.

Tom Mitchell was one of very few Indians to ever hunt the shaggy white monarchs. Having grown up in a cabin at the

From Dawn Until Dusk

*Tom Mitchell with a nice billy taken
in Montana's Mission Mountains.*

---

foot of Saint Mary's peak, near the southern end of the Mission range, he could see goats from his home, albeit miles away and thousands of feet up.

Though Tom was the provider of elk and deer meat for his family, his first obsession was hunting goats. He was one of those rare hunters who had the fortitude to regularly climb the seven thousand feet necessary in order to hunt them.

When I knew Tom he was an eighteen-year-old high school

student, tall and lean and athletic, with chin whiskers shaped like a goat's beard. Timid and quiet in human company, he yodeled and sang with vigor when alone on the windswept mountain ridges.

Tom's reputation as a great mountaineer was well known, and his skills as a goat hunter were legend. After Tom came to the dental clinic for treatment, I was invited to visit his home. The simple, rough-planked cabin was neat and clean and filled with goat heads and horns. Bearskin rugs lay on the floors and the walls were hung with eagle claws and feathers, elk and moose antlers. Tom's family wasn't rich financially, but they were very wealthy in other ways.

I asked Tom if I might be included the next time he went hunting in the peaks. His big grin sealed the agreement.

We planned a three day climb in early September, giving me a few weeks to get ready. I borrowed an aluminum pack frame and a down sleeping bag and put together the gear I thought I would need: broken-in boots, sturdy trousers and shirt, a light down jacket, and a rifle in case of bears. I wished I could have been included in the actual hunt, but not being a member of the tribe this was not permitted

The day finally arrived. Euni drove us to our starting point on the east shore of Saint Mary's lake. From there it was a near-vertical shot to our destination.

Tom's gear was very basic. His pack was military issue, with an old wooden frame, and his bedroll was simply two heavy quilts from his bed at home. He carried an old military .303 Enfield rifle with open sights, unsuitable for long range shooting.

We waved goodbye to Euni with arrangements for a pickup late Sunday evening, three days ahead. Euni shed a tear for me because she thought the wilderness would eat me. She feared she'd never see me again.

Tom carried a heavier load, but we hadn't gone far before I realized that he was at no disadvantage. In fact, I began to wish it was much heavier. As I toiled and sweated, he skipped and sang up and down the near-vertical slope, soon disappearing far up ahead. Just as I was sure he had left me to die he came jogging back to see what was keeping me. Then he was gone again. This was the program for the day. He would run back or I would spot

From Dawn Until Dusk

him sitting in a berry patch or posing on a rimrock far above.

I struggled along at a steady pace despite growing blisters and cramping muscles. After what seemed a lifetime of suffering and extreme exertion—not to mention some hair-raising cliff climbing—we finally broke free of the timber and brush and emerged into the glory of the high country. Compared to Tom I was fat and out of shape, but we had climbed almost seven thousand feet in a little over five hours.

After a few moments spent relaxing and savoring our accomplishment, we proceeded to climb up into an almost-level alpine meadow at the base of a gigantic snowfield. Here we dropped our packs. For the next three days this would be our home.

Since I was beat and sore-footed and wanted to go no further, I volunteered to set up camp and cook some food while Tom went on to the peak some five hundred feet above us to scout the country and look for goats. I spread our beds in the moss of the tundra, melted water from the snow pack, and heated some canned stew.

As I relaxed, I thrilled at a beautiful sunset—but soon began to worry about Tom. Where was he now? Dark was coming fast And I wasn't happy at the prospect of spending a night alone in grizzly country—or searching for his body at the bottom of a cliff.

As stars began to appear and the wind calmed, I heard the beautiful notes of a mountaineer's yodel floating down from the peaks. Outlined against the darkening sky, this amazing young man sang out his happiness and joy to the world below. He yodeled once again then came bouncing down the ridge and was in camp just like that.

He excitedly reported several goats just over the ridge. He thought we should be able to find them again at first light. While we talked, a huge mule deer buck in full velvet came out of the timber below and drank from the brook of snow melt. Further down in the timber, a bull elk whistled and grunted. For a young sportsman seeing all this for the first time, there could have been no more perfect moment.

We settled down, content, even with tired muscles and blistered feet. Our guns were by our sides and I had a flashlight.

Tom had passed along several grizzly stories as we climbed, and I had become increasingly wary. He'd told me of the time a year earlier when he had knelt to drink from an alpine pool, only to see the reflection of a charging grizzly. He had rolled to the side as the bear roared past. He'd then run downhill, dodging aside each time the bear almost had him. The bear finally grew discouraged, and retreated, grumbling. Tom had been pretty shook up, and had come to have quite a respect for the big bears.

I was thinking of bears as I dropped off to sleep—and I'm sure he was as well. Minutes or hours later, I was awakened by a noise behind me. The growling and gnashing of teeth. My hair stood on end. I was petrified, and for a moment couldn't move. Gathering my courage, I remembered the gun and flashlight. I decided to turn quickly, shine the light, and shoot the bear before it could attack. I knew I had to kill him instantly because I couldn't get out of the bag quickly enough to escape.

I gathered myself, rolled over, and shined the light—right in the face of a big old porcupine contentedly chewing the straps off my pack. What a relief! As my heart dropped out of my throat, however, my relief soon changed to concern. We still had a problem. He was ruining my pack in his quest for salt. What to do? If I chased him away he would just come back—and there were no trees from which to hang the pack. I had to shoot him.

I leveled the .30-30 and pulled the trigger. At the shot, the whole mountaintop erupted. I had forgotten Tom in my excitement, and when I shot he went into orbit. His scream could have been heard for miles. When I shined the light toward him, his quilts were drifting down like parachutes. Tom was nowhere to be seen, but soon his white face peered at me from over some bushes way down the mountain. "What in the world are you shooting at? You scared the crap out of me."

When I told him "a porky," he walked back into camp giving me an evil eye. He didn't say anything else, but I felt bad for the inadvertent scare.

With morning all was forgiven. We ate a breakfast of cakes and eggs, staring out over the Swan River valley and into the peaks of the Bob Marshall Wilderness. The valleys were filled with mist and fog and the mountains were glistening islands in the sky. No one in the world was awake to see this except for us.

From Dawn Until Dusk

After we ate, Tom and I shouldered our rifles and began the ascent to the top of Saint Mary's peak. My feet and muscles were quite sore but were soon forgotten with the elation of reaching the roof of the world. At the top Tom pointed out a small pile of rocks and explained that each person who conquered a major peak like this one was entitled to carve his name and date on a stone and place it on the monument. There were twenty or thirty stones on the pile, but I still felt part of a very select group.

We now began our hunt in earnest. Hiking down the rugged and narrow ridge to the northwest, we soon began to notice many tracks and beds in the steep shale slides. There were also tufts of white wool on the rocky outcrops and in the low brush. As we rounded a small peak on the ridge we came face to face with a large group of nannies and kids. They stared in surprise, standing for several minutes before moving cautiously down into the cliffs below.

Moving on, we were soon able to look into a large basin one thousand feet or so below us. It appeared inaccessible, surrounded as it was by cliffs on three sides and a vertical precipice below its outlet. Though it was early September, the water was still half frozen. We began glassing for goats in the basin and surrounding cliffs. Soon we had counted twenty-seven different animals, including one female with long arching horns that appeared to be at least thirteen inches long.

There were apparently no billies, although at this point I had a hard time distinguishing between male and female. Tom explained that billies were much larger and their horns thicker, but unless there were females and males together it was very tough to tell them apart. Billies also tended to be loners, preferring to live alone or in very small groups with no kids.

We were in no hurry, and the goats, being so far away, were unconcerned about us. The basin at first appeared totally inaccessible, but as we studied it more thoroughly it seemed that the ledges at our feet might stair step down into the shale slopes below. We decided to give it a try.

We carefully worked our way down. It seemed we were going to make it until we came to a drop off that was just a little too high. It would have been easy going down but impossible coming up. The goats in the basin were safe from intrusion. We retraced our steps back to the ridge and continued on around to the west.

By now my feet were a real problem. The blisters had long since burst and I could feel blood squishing as I walked.

From the next peak on the craggy mountaintop we spotted two large billies skylined down the ridge about a mile further west. This seemed a good time for me to remove my battered boots and give my tortured feet and muscles a rest. I volunteered to watch his stalk from this vantage point.

The mountaintop had very little cover for the stalk. Fortunately, goats aren't normally too concerned with danger as long as the threat seems far away. They see everything and keep their eyes on any potential threat, but don't react until that threat comes close. These billies were no exception. Tom was within four hundred yards before the goats became nervous. When he was within three hundred yards they began to move off around the mountain. I watched as he quickly lay down and took a rest on the rocks. At the shot, the goats bolted and began to run, but within a few dozen leaps one of them began to drop behind, obviously hurt.

When Tom realized the goat was hit he started after him. He ran and jumped across the boulders and ledges as nimbly as the goats. Unbelievably, he soon began to overtake them. The wounded goat was hit in the front leg, but was slowed hardly at all; it certainly would have survived the injury. Tom ran until he was a stone's throw behind the wounded goat—then he stopped and fired point-blank to finish him off. He had actually run down the slightly-injured animal—a feat I wouldn't have believed had I not seen it.

Hurriedly I placed my wounded feet back into the bloody boots and scrambled down the ridge to help him skin and dress his trophy. By the time I reached him he already had the head and skin off. With a big smile he posed for me as I approached. The goat was a fine trophy with nine-and-a-half inch horns. The growth rings showed him to be eleven years old—near the end of his natural life span. The boned-out meat was wrapped in the hide for transport back to camp and later off the mountain.

Darkness was again approaching as a very weary and hurting dentist and a fresh and energetic Indian reached camp. After a few bites of food and lots of water we soon were in our bags and fast asleep. No fear of bears or porcupines were likely to disturb

From Dawn Until Dusk

our rest this night.

Next morning we slept late. The sun warmed us as we packed up and broke camp. The meat and hide made our loads much heavier, but we left the remaining canned food in a cache for Tom's next trip.

Coming down proved to be an even greater ordeal as I soon lost both heels off my boots. I slid and fell on rocks and brush. My heavy load made the falls more painful.

Euni and Tom's girlfriend were at the meeting spot right on time. They were all smiles until they got a closer look at me. From slipping and falling, my pants were just shreds hanging from my belt. I had removed my shirt and tied it around my waist to cover myself. My face and neck had burned and peeled until my skin looked like cornflakes. My lips were cracked, my eyes were bloodshot, and my feet were bloody.

When Euni saw me she ran up to me in a panic. What happened to you? Why doesn't Tom look like that? Of course Tom just smiled, looking as fresh as ever.

We all had a good laugh at my expense, but it took more than a week for me to recover. I even had to wear house shoes to work until my feet healed.

Future trips found me better prepared for the conditions. For most hunters a mountain goat hunt is a once-in-a-lifetime experience, but for Tom the mountains were a way of life. And the mountains became an obsession for me as well. I have returned many times to the high country above timberline.

Several years after our experience together, a married Tom Mitchell was injured in a logging accident. His crippled leg finally slowed him down.

Chapter 6

A Narrow Escape

Since my days with Tom Mitchell in the cliffs of the Missions, I have ventured many times into the high country for goats, learning over time that a goat hunt almost always carries with it a possibility for life-threatening danger.

There are a few rules a hunter always needs to keep in mind. First and foremost, you must always be cautious not to place yourself in a position from which you can't escape. A goat hunter should never attempt to descend through unfamiliar territory after a day of hard climbing. Fatigue will often tempt one to look for shortcuts, to climb down cliffs or chutes that would be impossible to climb back up. And if he later comes to a spot where he can't descend further, he is stuck. And stuck in the high country can easily mean death.

Just a few years after my experience with Tom, mistakes in the near-vertical slopes almost pulled the curtains on me. I was hunting alone in the remote canyons of the Mission Mountains and had spotted two billies high on a cliff across the canyon from me. To get close, I climbed down from my current position, crossed a glacial creek, and climbed back up a rock slide beside a glacier. After an hour or more I was directly below the goats'

From Dawn Until Dusk

One of several mountain goats Burl took in the Missions.

position but still out of range. If I moved directly up toward them, the cliff would block my view and I still wouldn't have a shot. My only chance was to angle up, back across the glacier, and hope they didn't spook.

After another several minutes and some hairy climbing I dug myself into the packed snow and ice and turned to look for the goats. One of the billies had disappeared but the second one was standing on an invisible ledge about four hundred yards across and above me. He looked like a trophy. I settled down into the snow and tried to steady the crosshairs. Because of my position, however, I couldn't get a rest. The shot was impossible. What should I do?

As I considered my options he began hopping along the cliff face. He'd soon be out of sight. My desperation spawned a bright idea. Quickly I repositioned myself behind my .270 rifle, nestling it down into the snow. By twisting my head and seating the gun into a drift, I was able to very precisely align the sight without transferring my trembling to it. I was not touching it at all except with my finger. I squeezed the trigger.

Big mistake! When I recovered my senses I was thirty feet

down the snow slide and my eyes were full of blood. That gun had done a number on me and I had an idiot mark that would leave a permanent half moon over my right eye.

After clearing my eyes and scrambling back to my gun I started to search for damage at the other end. The goat was down on the ledge but still alive. He briefly struggled to get to his feet, then lay quiet. I aimed as best I could and shot several times trying to finish him off, but couldn't hit him again.

I decided that he must be hit hard and dying because my shots didn't seem to disturb him in the least. Since further shooting seemed pointless I decided to climb up to where he was to finish him off. Scrambling through the snow-covered boulders, I looked up from time to time to be sure he was still there. When I was still far below him I looked up to see his white rump disappearing over the top of a vertical stone pinnacle. He was gone and there was nothing I could do about it.

Dejection and disappointment overcame me and I just sat down in disgust. All that effort and my one big opportunity had been lost—and that beautiful animal was hurt and possibly dying. If he were to die one consolation was that in nature nothing is wasted—the eagles and coyotes would make good use of the protein.

I sat and brooded for several minutes wedged against a big rock with my head in my hands—whipped and worn out. Finally deciding there was no future in sitting there freezing to death, I stood, picked up my rifle, and pointed my tired body downhill.

Before starting I glanced across the glacier to the rock face beyond. To my surprise the second billy was there, staring at me as calm and unafraid as could be. I lost no time dropping down into the snow and sighting across at him. At the shot the goat dropped in his tracks and lay in a table-sized patch of low brush at the top of a five-hundred-foot vertical drop.

The second cardinal rule of goat hunting? Be sure that you can retrieve your quarry. I had been in such a hurry to shoot that I had forgotten the rule, and now I was in a pickle.

As I studied the situation I discovered a slight goat trail across the glacier a hundred feet or so above me. It seemed to continue across the broken rock face to where the goat lay. After a short prayer I gathered my courage and started up the steep slope.

From Dawn Until Dusk

Retrieving a goat can be the most difficult part of the hunt.

To my surprise, getting to him was not as harrowing as I had expected. Within thirty minutes I had crossed the ice field, found a good ledge around the cliff, and sat with my fingers deep within his luxurious white fur. But he lay in a tight spot on a very steep slope. In order to skin him, I tied him off to the brush above—hoping the shrubs didn't uproot and drop us both off into space. As I worked I reflected on what a fool I was to get myself into such a dangerous situation—all alone and miles deep in the wilds of the Rocky Mountains.

With the skin finally off and with a heavy load of meat on my back, I started off the mountain. I struggled back across the cliff on the goat trail to the edge of the snowfield. In my fatigue, I then had another bright idea.

Why not sit on my rump and slide down the slope of snow and ice to the bottom, saving time and effort? It looked easy enough, and I reasoned I could control my speed with elbows and heels.

I positioned myself on the ice with my pack in one hand and rifle in the other, elbows down and heels ready. Pushing off, I felt an instant of exhilaration—just before the panic!

I was out of control from the start. The speed was just too much to handle. Rocks hidden in the snow began to do considerable damage to my posterior, but I couldn't stop. The landscape whipped by me on either side, fast and blurred.

My speed problem was soon solved, however, when I dropped into a crevasse in the ice.

Fortunately, the fissure was only about one yard wide. And somehow my rifle caught across the span of the crack. I hung there with a death grip on the maple stock, listening to a creek rushing somewhere far below. I looked down into a blue and white, near-vertical death trap. If I fell, my body would never be found. My wife and infant son would live their lives not knowing what happened to me.

With a strength I didn't know I had, I pulled myself up and out of the cold grave and onto the ice. Somehow I was still grasping the pack as well as my rifle. With great relief I inched my way off the glacier and sat trembling in the rocks, counting my blessings.

After several minutes of rest, I followed my previous path down through the rocks and brush, vowing to never break the rules of the hunt again—and I haven't. Not often, anyway.

Chapter 7

Sometimes the Bear . . .

The morning sky was just turning from gray to gold as I left my old Dodge dart at the trailhead leading into Gray Wolf Peak, deep in the Mission Mountains.

I was in my second year as a dentist for the Flathead Indians, and was filled with a lust for adventure that only a young man can know. I had left Eunice and little Mark sleeping, departing long before dawn with a plan to be deep in the mountains by shooting light. I was hunting goats, the shaggy white monarchs of these highest peaks.

The previous fall I had taken a small billy, and had nearly killed myself in the process. This time I was determined to take an old guy, but not risk my life doing it. Little did I know what the morning would bring.

As I hiked up the canyon, the steep walls and tall timber kept the trail as dark as night. I was a little spooked as I quietly slipped along. This was grizzly country, and the thought of meeting a silvertip on this dark and narrow trail was more than a little unnerving.

Suddenly the brush cracked off to my right, and three mule deer came bounding toward me. They veered to the side just as a blood-curdling scream echoed from behind them. I froze in place, too petrified to move. For several minutes, all was deathly silent. I stood there straining to see or hear whatever had made that fearsome sound.

As the sun began to peek over the ridge, it became light enough for me to see into the trees. Finally I found enough courage to slip forward, rifle loaded and ready. The deer had left deep prints in the wet soil. I backtracked them, and soon spotted another track—a mountain lion!

I had foiled his hunt, and the loud scream had come as he had voiced his frustration. Like a ghost he had slipped away without another sound, even though I had been within fifty feet of him when the deer had bolted.

Burl has taken a number of black bears in Western Montana.

From Dawn Until Dusk

My heart slowed to a nearly normal pace. Again I headed up the trail toward the goat cliffs. I had a long hike ahead. This time of year the goats lived high above timberline. The trail climbed gently for the first few miles, then became steeper and steeper, finally to disappear into the high basin at the head of the drainage.

I hiked for a couple more miles, following a narrow trail through intermittent aspen and alder brush. The valley floor was home to a healthy population of beavers, and their dams slowed the creek in several locations. One of the larger ponds had flooded the trail. I found a downed log to use as a bridge, but as I stepped onto the log I was startled to see a very large and very fresh grizzly bear track—going the same way I was headed!

Needless to say, it was now decision time. Should I turn tail and get the heck out of there, or should I go on?

Good sense told me to leave the bear alone—but when it came to hunting, I had never been accused of having good sense.

I had never seen a wild grizzly up close, despite having spent many hours looking for one the previous spring. I just couldn't walk away from this opportunity, even though I knew it was dangerous. In these close quarters I could get in big trouble very quickly.

I stood there for a few minutes, changing my mind at least three times. At one point I even started back, but after a few steps turned around again. I finally tightened my belt, chambered a cartridge, and started on up the trail.

The bear continued to follow the only reasonable path through the thickets, his tracks clear in the intermittent mud. I moved without sound, my senses tuned to every sound, sight, and scent. The hair on my neck just wouldn't lie down!

The bear was only minutes ahead of me, but as I approached the cliffs where the trail switch-backed up the steep mountain face, it seemed that he was running out of room. I was within a couple hundred feet of leaving the valley floor and could see the cliff face through the trees ahead ... when I caught a whiff of something strong and rancid.

I had never smelled anything quite like it. It had to be the bear! I stopped, expecting to be attacked any second. He was close, but where was he? The brush all around me was impenetrable, and the valley was deathly quiet. Even the birds were silent.

Very carefully I turned all the way around. Nothing. I did note, however, a climbable tree about fifty feet behind me. Turning back up the trail, I heard a noise ahead, and quickly raised my rifle, ready to fire. The rustling sound changed to a sharp cracking. My first thought was that he was charging from the brush. But the sound was stationary and emanating from the thick brush ahead and to the left.

Now I knew where he was but still couldn't see him. What was he doing? I listened for a few minutes, and finally determined that he was feeding. The sound I heard came from bones cracking. I eased up the trail, as close as I could get without leaving the path. Still I couldn't see a thing—even though he now seemed to be only thirty or forty feet away.

This was much too close for comfort, so I quickly and quietly retreated down the trail, backing up against the only tree in sight that I might climb.

With my back to the tree, I continued my vigil—watching and waiting to see what might happen next. After only a couple minutes he stopped chewing bones. It became totally quiet. And then he charged!

Crashing through the brush, he came roaring out to the trail—right where I had been standing not three minutes ago. He must of winded me, and now he was determined to get rid of this intruder. The hair on his back and neck was upright, and he popped his jaws as he swung his head back and forth, looking for me.

A beautiful, golden-blond bear, his head as big as a bushel basket. A true monarch of these mountains. *Ursus horrilibis*, the horrible bear.

I had already determined that at this range, if I were to shoot, I had to be sure of a quick kill. Otherwise, he could potentially get me before he died. A shot in the head or right behind the ear would drop him in his tracks. I quickly placed the crosshairs behind his ear and shot.

He dropped as I expected, but bounced immediately back up. And was gone! Nothing could move that fast—but he did! The brush crashed as he bounded up and out of the canyon. All was quiet again. I controlled my shaking, and moved up to where he had fallen—no blood, only some golden-tipped hair.

From Dawn Until Dusk

My first thought? Thankfully, he had run the other way. As fast as he had moved I would never have gotten a second shot—much less been able to climb the tree.

That morning occurred over forty years ago, when things were quite different in the hunting world than they are today. But the images of that morning are etched in my mind as clear as a photograph. I can see the crosshairs on the bear's neck, right behind the ear, and the four inches of beautiful hair. That .270 bullet just made him duck and fall, and didn't touch anything but hair. Today I am glad he lived to roam those beautiful peaks—hopefully until he died of old age.

After several minutes of weighing my options, I turned back down the canyon and retraced my steps back to the car, occasionally looking over my shoulder, expecting at any minute for the bear to come for me.

It was still quite early when I arrived back home. Euni was sleeping in later than usual. She roused as I entered the bedroom. I said, "I have a small problem."

"What's going on?"

"I shot at a grizzly up in the mountains. I may have wounded him, but he got away."

She knew as well as I did that other people hiked in those mountains, and a wounded bear was a serious hazard. The news upset her so badly that she fainted and fell back on the bed—the only time that ever happened to her in her life.

She quickly recovered, and we had a strategy council right there on the bedside. We both knew something needed to be done.

I had been reckless up to this point, but it wasn't smart for me to follow a wounded bear alone—a decision I had already made two hours before.

My closest friend in Saint Ignatius was a white doctor whom I had hunted with previously. He was my first choice for a backup. I jumped back in the car and sped up to his house. "Jack, I might have wounded a grizzly. Can you help me go after him?"

"Are you crazy? Hell no, I'm not going after a wounded grizzly."

Gee thanks. Not such a good friend after all.

I next thought of my closest Indian friend, and off I went to talk with him.

When I presented my problem to Cliff, his response was, "Let me get my gun."

Within two hours or so we were back at the site of my encounter and searching the ground for any indication of a wound.

The bear had broken so many saplings as he had roared away that his trail was easy to follow for the first hundred feet or so. He also had left tufts of hair in his path. But there was no blood. We followed his scuff marks up and around the mountainside until we were positive that he was not wounded.

With relief and some disappointment, we left the valley to its bears, lions, deer, elk, and goats. But I knew I would be back.

I learned several things that day, the most important being that a true friend is one that will be there for you in danger and trouble—no questions asked. "Thanks, Cliff!"

Chapter 8

Back to Montana

October 1969 found me and Dad, along with our friends Ron and Ray, traveling to Montana together. The tales of my two years spent in Western Montana had whetted their appetites—and I was extremely anxious to get back myself.

I had spent two full hunting seasons there in 1966 and 1967. But opening a new West Virginia dental practice in 1968 had required all my attention and time. But now I was able to travel back to the mountains that I had come to love.

Our plan was to spend two full weeks hunting, first in the Mission Mountains on the Jocko River divide (we had visions of huge bull elk) and then later to wherever our instincts led us.

My old Dodge truck with a camper was to be our transportation and shelter throughout our stay. For four men it was going to be a little crowded but warm, and with a dependably dry bed.

Our first campsite was under huge fir and tamarack just off the reservation along the Jocko, at about seven thousand feet of elevation. The peaks of the Missions to the north and the Swan range to the east provided a snowy panorama for our camp. The first morning, we woke to about five inches of soft, powdery snow. A previous camper had left a stack of firewood, and we were

The best time to fish for big brown trout in the West is often when they spawn in the fall.

entertained the first evening by a snow-white ermine playing hide and seek in the wood pile. He darted in and out of sight, with no apparent fear of us.

We optimistically headed out on foot into the vast expanse of timber-covered wilderness. Dad and I went south while Ron and Ray headed north. I had previously hunted here with Joe Wheeler and had taken two bull elk in two years. I fully expected to find another trophy.

After walking several miles in fresh snow, we had encountered only one set of elk tracks—obviously a large bull, but it was headed across Montana in a straight line. We also saw where a large mountain lion had been hunting the high ridges.

As we came into an old clear-cut above camp, a bunch of Franklin's grouse ran out before us. A grouse stew was too tempting, so we bagged four of them with rocks and sticks. The Indians call these birds "fool hens." If they flush at all, they will usually fly only to a low limb where they can be knocked off. Dad, who had spent a lifetime shooting at ruffed grouse back

From Dawn Until Dusk

home in West Virginia, had a hard time believing a grouse could be so dumb.

We came into camp to find that the other two weren't back yet, so we quickly cleaned the birds and put them on to simmer. Since we had an hour or more before dark we decided to explore another clear-cut down the creek below camp. Just a mile or so away, the forest opened into a beautiful basin of beaver ponds and meadows, scattered aspen and fir.

Dusk was coming; mist and fog rose over the beaver ponds. Deer tracks were everywhere. We expected to see a mule deer bounce out at any moment. But when a deer did burst from the willows, we were shocked to see a waving flag of a tail as it ran. A whitetail deer at 7,500 feet in the Mission Mountains?

We needed meat for our stay, so I suggested to Dad that he try stalking this deer. That was all the urging he needed, and off he went. Moving through the soft snow, he soon was out of sight in the mist and growing darkness. Within just a few minutes a shot echoed from the mountainsides. I hurriedly followed Dad's tracks through the tall grass and across a beaver dam to where he knelt over a big whitetail doe. He already had it opened, and soon the field dressing was complete. Since it was close to camp, we hung the carcass above where it lay, removing only the hind quarters to carry back immediately.

For the next five days we ate well, and had a great time hunting through the vast wilderness of peaks and timbered valleys, but we saw no game except several more whitetail does. Finally we decided to leave this beautiful area and relocate to hopefully a more productive site. Since we still had ambitions for elk, we decided to move west to an area along the Bitterroot divide near Thompson Falls, another spot I had visited and with which I was somewhat familiar.

Late the next day we were in the new area, ready and anxious to try again. This country was different in that the timber was unbroken—vast areas with no parks or openings at all. We could only hope to stumble upon elk at close range, and shoot fast! There were plenty of elk here—tracks and droppings littered the ground, and several times we heard animals crash off in the trees ahead—but after three days we had seen nothing. Our time was now half gone, so we decided to move east for mule deer and antelope. Elk would have to wait for another year.

Our antelope permits were for the high prairie country east of the Crazy Mountains in Central Montana. Before dark we were driving south from Two Dot, Montana. Finding a lonely ranch turnoff, we parked and sacked out, hoping to find a good hunting place tomorrow.

After a leisurely breakfast in the camper, we drove on—this time looking for antelope. All this country was private ground, and we were surprised to see "No Hunting" signs posted everywhere. Antelope loafed on both sides, and several big bucks stared at us across the sage flats—all protected by posted signs.

In desperation we finally decided to ask anyway, and drove into a ranch yard. A large yellow sign in the driveway said, "No Hunting—Don't Ask."

The rancher was working on a baler near the barn. With a smile and apology I introduced myself—and then asked him if there was anywhere in the area we might hunt antelope and mule deer.

"You aren't hunting whitetails?"

"No, we have whitetails back home, we just want to hunt antelope and mule deer."

"Well, you can hunt right here. We need to get rid of a bunch of those critters."

With thanks, and after directions, I returned to the truck and gave the good news to the rest. We were in!

We drove through the ranch yard and pasture to the buttes and timbered hills beyond. Our excitement was hard to contain. Antelope seemed to be everywhere, and the rancher actually wanted us to kill them.

He had suggested we camp on top of a low butte near the middle of his property. We were approaching the butte when I spotted three antelope just below the rim, and one was a good buck. With no comment I drove on up the winding road and finally to the flat top of the hill. We parked near a windmill-powered well and stepped out to stretch.

Casually I suggested to Ron to get his rifle and come with me. He had not seen the three antelope and didn't suspect what I had in mind. As we approached the edge above where I expected to find them, I had Ron wait while I crept up to look over. Sure enough, they were grazing quietly just a hundred yards or so down the hill. Acting unconcerned, I motioned for Ron to crawl up to me. When he saw the tall black horns he nearly came unglued.

He quickly took a rest and fired. Too quickly! He missed completely. But the buck didn't know where the noise had come from. He ran up the hill toward us, stopping at fifty yards. Ron missed again. This time the buck spotted us. He sprinted off the hill at full speed and was soon streaking across the flat below. By the time Ron was ready to fire again, the buck was making dust over three hundred yards away. But at the shot he tumbled head over heels and lay still.

Ron stood up, stretched, and nonchalantly said, "Like the Sundance Kid, they have to be moving."

While we dressed and hung Ron's antelope, Dad and Ray had set up camp. We were ready to go hunting again. We headed back toward the timbered hills.

Less than a half mile out, a huge herd of antelope came running across above us. Ray was closest to them, less than two hundred yards away, and he quickly readied to shoot. He dropped to a prone position as they ran along a fence line parallel to him. There were fifty or more, with several good bucks, and they were running flat out—something had spooked them pretty bad.

Ray started shooting. Soon one antelope tumbled down. The bunch then turned and came down toward us, running behind a low hill. They stopped out of sight. They had to come out eventually, so I lay down and waited. Soon they began filing out at a walk on the hillside across from us. When a big buck stepped out, I held on the top of his back and squeezed off. Hair flew as if a pillow had been burst on his back. Away he went! I thought he'd been at least three hundred yards out when in fact he was only half that far. The whole herd burst out and over the hill, and I didn't get another chance.

We went up to help Ray. He admitted that he had hit a buck twenty or thirty feet behind the one at which he had actually been shooting. Nevertheless, two down and two to go. The rest of that day was spent taking care of capes and meat—and relishing our quick success.

Next morning, as Dad and I headed back into the hills, we saw deer in all directions, but no big bucks. Sixteen does in one group, then spikes and forkhorns. We had resolved to shoot only big bucks.

After lunch Dad and I worked the face of a long hillside. He went low while I quietly moved around above him. We hadn't gone far when I spotted a little doe lying just ahead and above him. I decided it would be a neat joke to spook her out to run past Dad. Chuckling I took a rest and aimed at a big rock just above her. I shot, and hit the rock right where I aimed. The doe didn't move. She just lay there, but now her head was down. Pretty smart animal to hide instead of run.

Dad couldn't see me, so he moved on around out of sight. Curiously, I slipped down toward the doe, and approached where I thought she was hidden. I crept along as slowly and quietly as possible, eventually spotting her through the branches. She hadn't moved!

Congratulating myself for my stalking skills, I stepped out and clapped my hands. Still she didn't move. With a sick feeling I walked up to her, and sure enough my bullet had obviously ricocheted—and broken her neck. After all that talk about big bucks, I had killed a doe. I was in for it now!

She was legal, however, and I still had a second tag for my big buck. I carried her into camp and took all the ribbing the guys could dish out. I deserved it.

We never did find any big muleys on that ranch, but the next day Dad had a great antelope hunt. Dawn found us on the rim glassing the distant flats. Before long we spotted an exceptional buck in a large group of does a mile or so away. Given the open, level country all around him, he seemed unapproachable. As we studied the situation, however, we finally decided that we might be able to get close by hiking up a shallow draw that meandered across the flat.

Dad would make the stalk while I watched through the spotting scope. We planned arm signals if needed, and he was off.

Dad disappeared off the rim to circle around, and I didn't see him again for two hours. I watched and waited, worrying that something might have happened. Had he gotten bit by a rattlesnake? Or maybe had a heart attack?

From Dawn Until Dusk

The antelope were still there and the buck had lain down.

Finally I spotted an orange spot, right in the middle of the antelope herd. I zoomed to forty power and focused in. It was Dad. But no sooner had I identified him than he disappeared again. For the next several minutes his head would be up, then down, then up again. I could see his problem was finding the buck. The buck was lying down, surrounded by does, and Dad couldn't see him. He had made a fantastic stalk, right into the middle of the herd, but now he was stuck.

Finally the buck stood up, and I saw Dad's gun come into position. I focused again on the buck, and suddenly he just fell over. Given the distance and wind, I never heard the report, but watched Dad as he walked over to the downed pronghorn.

I rejoiced on Dad's behalf, and then ran back over to camp for the Honda Trail 90. I started the little motorbike and zoomed off the butte to help Dad. He'd taken a great trophy. The horns were over fifteen inches, and had an inch of ivory at the tips.

Since big mule deer bucks seemed to be scarce at this ranch, we decided on another move. This time we would go to the badlands country south of the town of Ingomar.

We found a great campsite, miles from the nearest house, in a little dry valley where there had once been a school or church. Only the concrete foundation remained, an excellent place to park the camper. This was mostly public ground, with not a single posted sign, and we seemed to have it all to ourselves.

Next morning we fanned out to hunt the dry washes that cut the prairie like giant spider webs. Dozens of deer, both whitetails and mule deer, bounced out of the scant cover in the draws. Grouse flushed ahead of us every few minutes. I bagged one sharptail by shooting under it. The concussion of flying dirt knocked it cold without making a single hole in its skin.

The weather had become quite cold. We were now nearing the middle of November, and it was only ten above zero with a thirty-mile-an-hour wind. The deer stayed in the cover of the creek bottoms. Around noon Ron and I jumped a big whitetail buck, but he stayed in cover to make his escape.

Just before dark, as we slowly hunted our way back to camp—

Ron in the creek bottom and me on the side hill—a group of mule deer jumped out ahead of Ron and ran up the other side of the coulee. Hearing the commotion, I hurried to an outcrop and flopped down for a rest. It was almost dark, but through the scope I could make out the gray animals moving through the sage. Carefully inspecting each animal, I could see no antlers—then they started across the ridge. For just a few seconds each deer was skylined. I had decided there were no bucks when the last deer stepped into view. There he was, tall and wide. But I was too slow to recover. I centered the crosshairs and squeezed—but the safety was on. Then he was gone.

This was by far the best buck we had seen in two weeks, and I told Ron as we walked into camp that we would find him again, even if we had to walk all day. We told the others about him as well. Tomorrow would be our last day of hunting, and he was our last, best chance for a trophy deer. One of us had to find him!

Dawn was again cold and windy, but we tucked our chins and began to work every dry wash in the direction the deer had gone. By mid-day we were all separated and spread over several miles of prairie. I didn't know if the other guys had given up, but I was determined to search until dark. All day I had seen nothing but does.

With dusk I trudged, dejected and footsore, across the flats toward the camper. I had almost given up, but then I noticed one last dry wash off to my left that I hadn't seen before. It required a couple hundred yards of detour but I quickly decided to look into this final hole.

As I had so many times all day, I approached the rim as stealthily as possible. But this time, when I gazed into the dry coulee, antlers appeared just over the rim. He knew I was there, even though he couldn't see me. I could tell by the antlers he was alert and looking directly toward me. He was lying down, but a single jump would carry him down and out of sight. I had one chance, and I had to be quick.

I eased back one step, flipped the safety, and with the rifle to my shoulder stepped forward. Our eyes met, and then he went airborne even as my shot echoed across the plain. He collapsed into a heap at the bottom of a twelve-foot hole.

Whooping and hollering, I forgot for a minute how tired I

From Dawn Until Dusk

was. My strategy worked after all. It just took a little longer than I had planned.

I jumped into the hole and started to dress him out. A very difficult place to work, but after wrestling him around I finally had him cleaned. I stood up, and there was Ron looking down at me, a big grin on his face. "Man, you sure are slow. I was getting tired of watching you wrestle that thing."

It was a relief to see him. I'd had already decided I could never get this big buck out of the hole without help. It proved to be a real challenge even for two us.

Our first hunt West was now over, and we each had a trophy to remember it by. We had a great time, and resolved to do it again next year. We did in fact do it again the next year, and for many years after.

Montana has changed dramatically since 1969. On that trip we saw not one other hunter in the field. Things are tougher now, but the big sky is still there, as are the big bucks.

Chapter 9

What the Magpies Said

In the fall of 1971, I traveled with my dad and old friends Ron, Ray, and Vernon Taylor to Western Wyoming and the mountains above the famous Pitchfork Ranch. Well into our hunt we'd already bagged a nice bull elk and a trophy-class pronghorn. But then we spotted a group of huge mule deer bucks.

Dad, Ron, and I had walked eight or ten miles that morning. We stopped on a barren slope to glass the pockets of timber across from us. The wind was bitter but the sky was clear. The sun sparkled on a light snow covering the ground. Five or six hundred yards away, a mule deer buck fed above a small pocket of timber. He was a beauty, with a wide, heavy rack and thick body.

Since Dad had never shot a trophy mule deer, Ron and I volunteered to stay behind and signal to Dad as he made the stalk. Immediately after he left us, we spotted a second buck lying at the edge of the timber below the first one. As Dad dropped into a gully out of sight, the first buck spotted us. It spooked and ran down into the timber. The second buck followed him. When they ran through the timber and out the other side, they were followed

From Dawn Until Dusk

by at least ten other big bucks and some smaller ones. They all ran across an open flat and disappeared into Jack Creek Canyon.

None of us had ever seen such a spectacle before. The day was getting late, and the deer had headed north (camp was south). We walked toward home with the vow to return tomorrow.

Next morning, Dad, Ray, and Vernon decided to hunt closer to camp, but Ron and I hiked back to our previous spot, seeing visions of the big bucks in Jack Creek Canyon.

Our strategy was to drive through the many small pockets of timber, one guy posted in a position to shoot an escaping animal and the other guy silently hunting through the trees, hoping to catch a buck in his bed.

The first pocket was high above where we had seen the bucks yesterday, but it looked promising. I posted and Ron circled, silently entering from the far side. He had just entered the timber when a small bull elk emerged and, looking back over his shoulder, passed below me. Next came two small, three-point bucks and a doe, followed quickly by Ron.

I drove the next pocket with similar result. Does and fawns emerged, followed by a scraggly coyote. No shooting for Ron.

Next was a pocket just above where we had seen the bucks yesterday. It was Ron's turn to drive. I watched him disappear into the trees as I sat behind a boulder and found a rest for my rifle. I just knew something was going to happen. I soon saw Ron slipping through the trees toward me—but nothing had come out. Disappointed, I stood up and waved, just as a beautiful buck raced out of the timber. He was already more than one hundred and fifty yards away and covering twenty feet at a jump. I shot several times at him. On the last shot, just as he disappeared into the trees, he seemed to stagger.

Ron came around the hill. "Did you miss him?"

"I don't think so."

We gave the buck a few minutes to catch his breath then went down to where he had ducked back into the timber. There were lots of tracks in every direction in the snow—but no blood.

This pocket was where all the bucks had been yesterday. The snow was so tracked up that trailing was impossible. We searched for a couple of hours but in the absence of blood I began to doubt I had hit him at all. Probably he had simply stumbled or slipped

Left to right, Ray, Burl's dad Opa, Ron, Burl, and Vernon.

on the ice. Finally we gave up and hunted our way across the open mountaintop back to camp.

That evening I kept thinking of that buck and the way he had staggered on my last shot. Finally Ron and I decided to hunt over that way again the next day. By noon we were searching the patch of timber in a systematic grid. Two hours later, still no luck. Nothing was dead or alive in that dark timber except for a few squawking magpies. Again we hunted our way back to camp without seeing any deer at all. We were beginning to think we had scared everything out of the country. But then Ron spotted a small group of antelope on a flat below us. Antelope at ten thousand feet—a big surprise. We stalked to within one hundred yards or so, but passed up the fourteen-inch buck with hopes of finding a better one closer to camp.

Over grouse stew that night we discussed the events of our last two days and the beautiful, game-rich country surrounding us. Ray described seeing a mountain lion kill just a mile above camp. A big mule deer buck, partly eaten, had been buried in the dirt and pine needles. We all agreed this was a hunter's paradise. We

From Dawn Until Dusk

had seen and bagged antelope, elk, grouse, and mule deer—and now we knew a mountain lion lived here as well.

As we relaxed around our campfire my thoughts returned to my lost mule deer trophy . . . and I had a revelation! "Ron, we've got to go back there again. I know we can find him now." The magpies had told me. The cantankerous, black-and-white birds had been flying in and out of a deep tangle that we hadn't investigated. "That's where he is." I kicked myself for being so blind.

Ron was dubious, but as usual he was game for anything. At dawn we were on our way again. This time I was anxious to test my theory and we made record time. By 10:30 we were in the timber and zeroing in on magpie chatter ahead. As we approached they flew out, but we had the spot pinpointed. We forced our way into the dark tangle. At first we saw nothing but tracks and bird poop, and then I spotted an antler!

The buck had fallen under a log with only part of his rack visible. We dragged him out and inspected the ruined carcass. He had been hit twice—once high on the back with little damage and once in the lower jaw. As we looked around we discovered he had bled extensively just a few feet back from where he had fallen. I think the broken jaw had eventually cut a major blood vessel while he had run through the brush. Further back we could find no blood at all.

Though time and magpies had ruined the meat, I salvaged the antlers and proudly lashed them to my pack for the long hike back. This buck was a dandy—my best ever. I was elated we had finally recovered him. Once again persistence paid off.

Chapter 10

The Far North

Every sportsman dreams of an adventure into the wilds of Africa or Alaska. I have been blessed to experience a number of these wonderful hunts, but the most memorable was the first.

While reading an outdoor magazine in the winter of 1970, I noticed an article about Canada's Northwest Territory. What impressed me most was that this huge country had been opened only the year before to non-resident hunting. It remained a vast, untouched wilderness. There had been some light aerial exploration for oil and minerals, but for the most part not even the Indians had seen much of this country. It was too far inland for the coastal tribes, and too far north for most of the inland groups.

The article described the large moose and caribou in the area, and the huge numbers of Dall sheep, most of which were dying of old age. For a dreamer like me this sounded like the opportunity of a lifetime.

I wrote the government of the Northwest Territories for information on hunting licenses and a list of outfitters. The reply was prompt. The all-game license was only $150, with no additional trophy fees. The entire Northwest Territories had only

From Dawn Until Dusk

seven licensed outfitters, dispersed across an area comparable in size to the United States west of the Mississippi. Wow!

After corresponding with all the outfitters, I chose to go with Zane Palmer. His exclusive hunting area encompassed over seven thousand square miles of mountain peaks and pastures in two major river drainages—and was one of very few that offered horseback hunting. His base camp was on Palmer Lake in a divide between river drainages.

Having done all the research, I called my good friend and hunting partner, Ron. "Want to go on a wilderness trek and hunt moose, caribou, sheep, and grizzly in pristine country for about $2,500, including license and transportation?"

"Let me get my boots on. When do we leave?"

Our hunt was set for the first two weeks of September, 1973. The sheep would be getting their winter coats, moose and caribou would have shed their velvet, and the moose would be starting their rut.

As the date approached, the anticipation was nearly too much to bear. An adventure like this was unimaginable for two hick kids growing up poor in the hills of West Virginia. But now it was actually going to happen.

On August 28 Ron met me at my home near Charleston, West Virginia, and we caught our flight out next day. From Charleston we flew to Toronto, Edmonton, and finally north to Norman Wells, Northwest Territories, on the east shore of the mighty McKenzie River. At that time Norman Wells was accessible only by plane, the nearest highway ending over one thousand miles south. The airport was fairly busy as this was becoming a hub for the growing oil and gas industry of the far north.

Even though the landing strip could accommodate large jets, the terminal reminded me of a cow-pasture port in the states. A one-room steel building with a single attendant greeted us as we packed our own gear from the plane into the building.

As it was obvious no one was there to greet us, we asked the guy behind the counter, "Do you know how we can get in touch with Zane Palmer?"

"Who?"

"Zane Palmer."

"Never heard of him."

"He's an outfitter, and was supposed to meet us here today."

"Are you sure you got off at the right place?"

This conversation went on for several minutes, with Ron and I becoming increasingly nervous. We decided to sit down and wait it out. We couldn't do anything else.

About thirty minutes later, as we were beginning to doze off on our bags, a guy in a big cowboy hat poked his head in the door. "Anybody here for Palmer Lake and points west?'

Zane was a nice-looking, mild-mannered gent about thirty-five-years-old. Confident and capable, he never mentioned nor apologized for being late. Tight schedules just don't seem to apply in the far north. Before we left, however, we did introduce him to the clerk.

Two hours later, after some errands and mail pickup in town, we loaded our duffles and rifles into his vintage, single-engine Otter. It bobbed off his makeshift dock, tilted in the water over leaky floats. Ron and I looked at each other doubtfully. We were flying in that? Zane poured oil into the engine and pumped water out of the floats. He assured us that since the plane had flown for over thirty years already, one more day wouldn't be an issue. When I asked him about the film of oil down the side of the plane, he just said, "No problem."

We piled in on top of the gear, taxied across to the far shore, turned, and roared away—almost clipping the tree tops as we went. Zane circled for altitude while Ron and I thrilled at the vista around us. The river was several miles wide, with vast tundra to the north and east and beautiful blue mountains to the west.

Leveling off across the wide McKenzie, I glanced at the gauges. None of them seemed to work—not even the compass! If we were to go down on the west side of this huge river, we'd never be able to get back across. If necessary, I supposed we could build a shelter from logs and driftwood. Eat moose and fish. With a little luck we could survive the winter, maybe.

By this time we had crossed the water and were winding through the narrow valleys between gigantic, barren peaks. Occasionally we could see white dots on the slopes. Zane said they were sheep. Soon all thought of danger was gone. Ron and I began to enjoy the scenery and the thrill of having our adventure finally begin.

From Dawn Until Dusk

After roughly 150 miles of flying, we caught a glimpse of a beautiful, sapphire-colored body of water ahead. Palmer Lake. As we made our approach, the white wall tents on shore came alive with activity. The landing was perfect and we soon taxied to shore. The native guides approached and, after hurried greetings, secured the plane to the dock and unloaded our gear and groceries. In broken English, they began to tell Zane about a grizzly in camp. Soon they were pointing to sheep on the slopes above camp and telling us about the great fishing in the lake.

Our guides, Lee and Eddie, were Indians of the Beaver Clan from the Fort Saint John area of British Columbia. They were new to this area and were quite excited about the quality of the big game animals here. We soon learned that even though Zane was in his fourth season here, he had not needed to go more than ten miles from base camp to fill out all his hunters—in an area of seven thousand square miles! The rest was virgin and untouched territory.

Mrs. Palmer suggested we go catch some fish for supper and unwind from our trip. She produced two worn-out casting outfits with rusty spoons and pointed to a rocky point about a hundred yards down the shoreline. Only one of the reels worked, but we weren't especially optimistic anyway. For Ron and me it had always been, "You should have been here yesterday." I insisted he go first.

His first cast was short, barely past the rocks, so he retrieved quickly to try again . . . but a fish grabbed the spoon before he could get it out of the water. He yipped in surprise and soon had the fish up onto the rocks—a four pound lake trout! We both thought this had to be a fluke, but on his second cast he immediately had another strike. Just as quickly the fish jumped and threw the spoon, but before he could crank it in, he had another fish on—this time a six pounder.

It was now my turn. After wrestling the rod from Ron, I caught two fish with two casts. These fish were all between four and six pounds, and within twenty minutes we had all the fish we could use. We carried our string up to the large cook tent and were assured that the fishing was always like this. Grayling were also in these waters, and before we left we caught grayling over eighteen inches from the floats of the plane.

Our guide Lee said, "Eat lots. Tomorrow you're going to need the energy."

Our guides understood English perfectly, but we had a hard time making out their thickly-accented responses. In their native language they joked and laughed. I'm sure they made fun of us—while we could only shrug and smile. They proved to be good guys and great guides, but the lack of conversation was annoying throughout our time together.

Early the next morning, we rode west down the broad, gravel-strewn river valley. Our caravan consisted of two hunters, two guides, and four pack horses carrying enough equipment and grub for a week in spike camp. We would be hunting about eight miles away. As we traveled down the valley we saw no game, but tracks were everywhere. Moose, caribou, grizzly bears, and wolves had been up and down the trails. We were already hearing wolves from afar, and we would continue to hear them every day and night. Their tracks were immense, as big as most of the bear tracks, but the animals themselves were like ghosts, almost never seen. We learned later that in most years none were killed by hunters, even though they were quite plentiful. We failed to catch even a glimpse of one in two weeks, but we often found their tracks inside ours from the day before.

Spike camp was set up by mid-afternoon along a meandering, glacial brook teeming with grayling. We camped in the short, gnarled timber. The trees were only substantial enough to provide a trace of cover for large animals and to give us just enough fuel for our campfire.

The horses were soon hobbled and turned loose in the tall, frost-burned grass. Tomorrow would find us on foot, climbing up the mountain behind camp for sheep. The horses would have a day or two off to regain their strength.

By the campfire, our guides told stories in broken English about huge moose and forty-six-inch rams, and Lee demonstrated his prowess with the camp ax. He threw it with perfect accuracy, and the blade always stuck where it hit. The ax was his knife and his weapon. He was never without it, and he kept it honed razor sharp.

The next morning dawned clear and frosty. The sun reflected off snow-capped peaks, sheep pastures on the high slopes, and

From Dawn Until Dusk

white sparkling frost. Breakfast consisted of hot bannock and cold fish from supper. We filled our packs with tea, honey, canned meat, and more bannock. We left camp and began our climb up the small stream by our camp. Soon the cliffs closed in on our path, and we were forced to cross the stream, then cross it again. The water felt colder than ice and was deep and strong in the narrow chutes of the canyon. Each crotch-deep crossing became another agonizing challenge. After removing his boots and pants for the first crossing, Ron and I decided the misery was lessened by leaving them on. The rocks and icy water were just too painful on bare feet. Lee removed his boots on every crossing and didn't seem to be bothered by the sharp, slippery stones or the frigid water.

A mile or so from camp the canyon began to widen, and we could see into some of the cliffs and pastures further up. Suddenly we startled a band of snow-white ewes and lambs drinking in the creek. This lifted our spirits considerably. Within a few hundred feet we were able to leave the creek and begin a mountain traverse. Now we could see most of the surrounding countryside, and Lee spotted four rams high up the mountain to our left, below a vertical face on a grassy bench. Quickly we set up the spotting scopes. They all looked like full curl rams, but Lee said none were in the forty-inch class we wanted. He seemed to feel confident, even though they were nearly two miles away.

Again we loaded up and started toward the top. Within an hour we were onto the grassy benches favored by sheep. Since it was now noon, Lee suggested we stop, build a fire, brew a pot of tea, and "eat lots." Sounded like a good idea. The climb had been invigorating and I had already been thinking about bannock and honey.

We rested and ate for thirty minutes or so before we were back on our feet and hunting again. No sheep could be seen as we traveled from one bench to another—each looking more promising than the last with numerous beds pressed into the shale slides. On each rise, we stopped to glass the country ahead.

Ron walked in the lead with Eddie; he had drawn first shot on sheep and needed to be in position in case we surprised something close. In this open country we expected to spot our game miles away, but as luck would have it two rams bolted from a small basin just ahead, running across a grassy slope toward the cliffs below. Immediately Ron opened up with his 7 mm magnum, emptying it as the rams rapidly widened the range. When he clicked on empty I handed him my rifle and he continued his barrage. On the last cartridge, with the rams about four hundred yards away, the largest ram dropped in a heap and didn't move. When we came up to him we found the wound just under the tail—dead center as he was going straight away.

Ron's ram was a beauty. He had unblemished, thirty-seven-inch horns and a perfect white cape. Ron was very happy with his trophy. After many photos and congratulations, and by the time we had boned the meat and removed the cape, it was getting late enough to head back toward camp.

As we dropped down to where we had spotted the first rams, we again searched the high slopes above us. They were still there, feeding contentedly. We set up the spotting scopes and carefully looked them over, this time in a different light and from a different angle. Lee had soon changed his story. "There's your ram. A little over forty inches. You want to go after him?"

As tired as I was, the news renewed my energy. "Let's go."

Ron and Eddie stayed behind to watch the show as Lee and I sweated up the steep mountainside toward the rams. We were racing darkness; my legs burned from the exertion. My legs cramped, and the last several yards were covered on hands and knees. Finally we bellied up to the rim and peered over. As we expected the four rams were still feeding, completely unaware of us. All were full curls but the largest was exceptional. With his wide flaring tips he was a good curl and a quarter.

The range was only one hundred yards. Without further thought I sighted the rifle at his shoulder and fired. He tumbled down the steep shale slide—and fell over an eighty-foot cliff. What had I done? We had them where they couldn't escape, yet I had shot where he could fall and possibly destroy those beautiful horns. As we approached I saw that one horn had broken off three or four inches of the tip and the other horn was cracked across the middle but still intact. The unbroken horn measured forty and one-half inches. While Lee caped and boned the meat I searched up the slope for the broken tip, but to no avail.

After the initial disappointment of the damaged horns I

From Dawn Until Dusk

Burl's guide, Lee, with Burl's exceptional Dall ram.

stopped to consider the beauty of my trophy, and the fantastic day we had experienced. I decided that if the hunt were to end there I could go home satisfied. We had taken two great animals, and on only the first day of our hunt.

By the time we rejoined Eddie and Ron, it was completely dark and they had a fire going. We had hot tea (more tea in one day than I normally drink in a year) and then proceeded down the canyon toward camp.

On one of the hurried creek crossings, an incident happened that I had been fearing since morning. I slipped on loose rocks and was doused over my head in the icy water. Embarrassed, I struggled to shore, wet and shivering but otherwise unharmed. In camp the down sleeping bags sure felt great, and we slept soundly until the sun drove us from our beds the next morning. The day was then dedicated to caping the heads and caring for the meat and skins—and of course cooking and eating. "Eat lots."

Much to my dismay, I discovered that both my cameras, my binoculars, and my spotting scope were all fogged from my fall into the icy water. They were ruined. That fall was more expensive than the entire rest of the hunt. I was determined, however, that this small problem was not going to ruin my time. Ron had a camera and a spotting scope, we had a bunch of good sheep meat—and tomorrow we were going moose hunting.

We were expecting the moose hunt to be easier, but it proved to be a wild-and-woolly experience. First we moved spike camp down and across the river, which proved to be an adventure in itself. Those glacial rivers are strong and wide, and riding a horse as he swims and lunges is no fun at all. Even perching high on the saddle, we were thoroughly soaked by the time each crossing was completed.

The moose hunt was primarily from horseback, with a lot of long-distance glassing. Our first day was uneventful. From more than a mile away, we spotted a wandering bull in the riverbank timber, but by the time we had moved down toward him he had disappeared. I was amazed at how quickly such a huge animal could evaporate into the sparse cover.

Next morning found us riding along the timber edge. Wide gravel bars separated us from the timber across the river. Suddenly a huge bull bolted from the trees, running like a wild mustang down the bar and then back into the timber. Lee spurred his horse and galloped across the river in a giant spray. He yelled back to Ron, "Come on!"

Ron's bronc needed no encouragement to follow Lee at breakneck speed, and the race was on to overtake the moose.

Ron had never been much of a horseman, and to hang onto that animal at full gallop through the river and then over giant boulders would have been a challenge even for a rodeo star. As the horse jumped and zigzagged, Ron flopped from one side to the other, desperately clinging to the mane and saddle horn. He looked like a trick rider as he bounced across the horse's back. Luckily he stayed on top and wasn't tossed into the rocks. When it became obvious the moose had eluded them, they meekly rode back. Eddie and I wiped the tears and held our sides. What a show! Too bad I had ruined my 8 millimeter movie camera.

Next came the customary pot of tea, the bannock and honey, and another, "Eat lots." We rode out from the river and up an incredibly long and wide valley. We were above timberline. It was completely open except for waist-high brush and a few stunted alpine fir. The horses were having a hard time struggling over

From Dawn Until Dusk

hidden boulders covered with knee deep muskeg. At each step they either stumbled on the rocks or sank into the muck between them.

Lee stopped and asked Ron for his binoculars. He had spotted a pair of bull moose two miles away across the valley in a high basin. With the binoculars, he declared that one was big enough. "Let's go." A man of few words. A small creek ran down through the valley, providing a path. We left the horses tied out of sight and, on foot, circled wide to approach the unsuspecting pair from above. The muskeg was murder to walk in and I felt even more sympathy for our horses.

Coming over the rim, we advanced one slow step at a time until we could see into the entire basin. No moose! Deciding we were in the wrong basin, we backtracked and swung around into the next one. Again we slowly advanced to the rim and looked over. Bingo! The smallest bull stood just below us. The big bull lay in the brush further down.

Ron looked over at me with a questioning smile.

"Your turn," I said. "Take him if you want."

"Looks good to me."

There seemed no way he could escape, so Lee stepped out yelling and waving his arms. The big bull jumped up. Both animals stood and stared. I'm sure they had never seen a man before. They weren't at all afraid.

Ron dumped the big guy with a perfectly-placed shot, and happily accepted congratulations all around. A very good trophy, fifty-six inches wide with good palmation. It would look great in his trophy room in Virginia.

Back in camp we had a long discussion about the rest of our hunt. We had been out a week now and felt we should change our area since we had seen very few moose, no caribou, and no bear. Eddie and Lee agreed, but said we would have to clear it with Zane first. So next morning Eddie and Ron left on the long ride back to base camp while Lee and I rode upriver, hunting.

We had been out of camp only a few minutes when I spotted a bear near an island of brush in the river bottom. Jerking the rifle from its scabbard, I jumped off my horse and ran to a boulder for a rest. The grizzly was nearly three hundred yards away and walking toward the brush. With a solid rest I was confident of the shot and settled the crosshairs at the base of his tail.

Lee didn't share my confidence. "Don't shoot" he exclaimed, grabbing my elbow. The bear stepped out of sight into the brush. He thought we could get closer. "Come on," he added, already running across the gravel bar toward the island.

We circled cautiously, ready for action. When the bear didn't show, we went back around and picked up his track. After entering the brush, he had apparently bolted across to the other side of the river. He'd known we were there all along.

It had been the trophy of a lifetime. The vision of his beautiful, golden-blond coat remains with me today. But that's why we call it hunting and not shooting.

Ron and Eddie didn't return that night, but at about 11:00 next morning they came down the trail with Ron singing *Country Roads*. Over tea, bannock, and honey, they told us the plan for our last five days. We were to pack back to base camp today, and tomorrow we would cross the divide and pack twenty-five miles down to the forks of the Mountain River.

Ron and Zane had flown yesterday evening, and had spotted three huge bull moose at the river forks, and several caribou in the hills above the river. They had never before hunted there so Ron and I were thrilled to be the first.

Back at base camp we had a good night's sleep and a great breakfast. Then we were off again on fresh horses for a very long ride . . . into virgin territory!

As we passed the limits of previous hunts there was no sign of human intrusion anywhere. We passed two cow moose with calves that stood and stared as we rode past. There were no trails. The brush and muskeg forced us to cross and recross the dangerous river. The packhorses were always trying to go back home or find an easier way.

When we finally reached the wide gravel bar at the river forks, dusk was fading to dark and we were all exhausted. But then a huge bull moose suddenly stepped into view. There was no doubt on this one. I found that I wasn't tired at all. As quickly as possible I was off my horse with my rifle in hand. I flopped in the boulders and squeezed off a shot. The range was over two hundred yards but he looked as big as a barn door in my scope.

From Dawn Until Dusk

With the crosshairs just behind his shoulder I squeezed off . . . but the animal didn't even flinch.

"You missed."

"No way."

I shot again at the same spot, still with no reaction. Had my scope been knocked off? I swung to the moose's shoulder and pulled off a third time. This time his knees buckled a little. He turned and galloped across the river and into the brush.

We rushed over to where he had been standing. He'd been so big none of us could believe it. Lee and Eddie had guided for many years but had never seen a bull even close to this one. His antlers had looked to be at least six feet wide, with palms like refrigerator doors.

We picked up his tracks in the sand and gravel but could find no blood. I waited at the spot where his tracks entered the water while Lee went back for the horses. While waiting I moved down along the water's edge and searched the timber on the far side with my eyes. Almost immediately I spotted him. An antler, then his head and neck. He was down, but his head was still up. The huge antlers looked unreal. Aiming for the neck, I shot again. And again, instead of falling, he jumped up and ran parallel to the riverbank, through the brush and timber. I ran down the other side, shooting every time he crossed an opening. Finally he fell on his nose and flipped over. This time he stayed down.

Lee and Eddie brought the horses over and we crossed to the downed bull. We stared in disbelief. The greatest bull any of us could imagine—and he was mine!

The horses were quickly unloaded and camp was pitched in the sand by the moose. We were camping with our fry pan ready and warming on the fire.

Next morning at first light, Ron and I were out and fondling those extraordinary antlers. The little tape measure I carried revealed the antlers to be sixty-eight inches wide with palms that were eighteen inches across and over four feet long—with fifteen points on each side. If my measurements were correct this was a new world record Canadian moose, scoring over 240 points. Months later his official score proved to be 239 5/8, breaking the old record by five-eighths of an inch.

On closer inspection, we found that each of my shots had

Burl's huge bull moose scored well enough to make it a new world record.

---

entered where I had aimed, and would eventually have been fatal. Given other wounds to his neck and shoulders, he had been fighting, and his adrenaline level must have been very high. He just didn't feel any of the seven shots from my .300 magnum.

With both our sheep and moose hunts complete, we had three days to concentrate on caribou.

From camp we could see a group of fifteen caribou a few miles up the mountainside. Through the spotting scope, there were two bulls that looked to be shooters. Leaving camp on horseback, it didn't take us long until we were less than half a mile below them. We stalked over the ridge and into the little basin . . . and right into the herd. The cows and calves ignored us but the bulls had disappeared. We backed off, and as we moved around to look over the next ridge a bull stood up from the brush beside the cows. Ron dropped to take a rest. He shot. And missed. Away they all went over the ridge.

Lee and I headed back down for the horses while Ron and

From Dawn Until Dusk

Eddie followed the caribou, hoping to get another chance. We were only about halfway back to the horses when a big caribou bull stood up in the brush ahead of us. A *really* big caribou bull! He bolted immediately, however, and ran down and across the wide basin below us. By the time I could dismount and get into position to shoot, he was nearly four hundred yards away and still traveling. I knew my chances were slim but I started blasting away. On the third shot he staggered and fell back down the hill. What luck. The last day of hunting and another wonderful trophy. He had great, spreading brown antlers and a snow-white cape.

After caping and boning the meat we rode up toward where the others had gone, and soon met them coming down. They had bagged the other bull and were ready for packhorses as well.

Ron and I hugged and congratulated each other once again. Good friends and a great time together. How much better could it be?

The next day was very long and full of tougher traveling than the trip in. The poor horses struggled with the antlers and heavy loads, and nearly bogged down numerous times. But finally we made it across the pass and into base camp for the last time.

At dawn we were up and packing for our flight out. Zane insisted that since our trophies were so large he would rather pack them out after his last hunt. With his assurances that we would see the trophies at the end of the season, we climbed into the Otter and waved our goodbyes to new friends.

I wish I could say that a few weeks later we received all our hard-earned trophies in great shape, but this wasn't to be. Zane had the misfortune of an early, deep snow and he lost several horses as he trailed out to Ross River. He said he wasn't able to get our trophies out that winter at all, and for some unexplained reason did not get them to us the next winter either.

Two-and-a-half years after our hunt, and after dozens of letters and phone calls, we finally received a crate from Zane. The crate held both moose antlers, our sheep horns and capes, both caribou capes, and Ron's caribou antlers. My beautiful caribou antlers were missing, and both moose capes as well. I have never recovered my caribou, but I have my memories.

Chapter 11

A Black Wolf in British Columbia

Our next great adventure was in northwestern British Columbia. Since Ron and I had both taken bighorn and Dall sheep, it was only natural for our thoughts to turn to stone sheep.

After much research and correspondence, we booked our hunt with an outfitter, "Don," out of Fort Saint John, hoping for stones and grizzly bear. We were assured by Don and his references that our chances were excellent for both species. Don reported an annual success rate of 60 percent on sheep, and bears were regularly taken too. Don also emphasized that his area was excellent for other species as well—especially moose and goat. We booked for the last two weeks of September in 1977.

We were met in Fort Saint John by Don's wife, and then drove up the Al-Can highway to milepost 146 where we were to meet Don and his super cub. A small bush strip alongside the highway was the hub for outfitter traffic in that area. About a dozen planes came and went before Don showed up. After quick introductions we were roaring off over the tree tops.

A thirty minute flight put us in base camp. It was quite a surprise to find such a beautiful valley containing his log lodge and several guest cabins. He owned three hundred acres here, with

From Dawn Until Dusk

fields and fences, barns and corrals, and a herd of forty or fifty horses grazing all around. This wasn't the primitive wilderness we had expected.

We were greeted by Don's older son, Rick, and the other guides, cooks, and wranglers. Don needed a large crew to accommodate his rotating groups of hunters—as many as eighteen or twenty at a time. We began to have doubts. How could we expect to find game in such a heavily-hunted area?

After stowing our gear in one of the cabins, we walked to the cook "shack" for our first meal. Moose steak with all the trimmings. While we ate we listened to Don tease us, his kids, and the other dudes. I quickly decided he was an arrogant and self-important man. After a few days I found that even his son didn't care for him.

The first phase of our hunt was to be for moose and bear. We'd be traveling on horseback out of base camp. The next morning we were up at dawn, ready for action. As we watched from our cabin, the wrangler chased a herd of horses in from the meadow. He caught and saddled some fat ones for our ride.

Ron and his guide headed north while Rick (my designated guide) and I headed east into a huge burned area. Not far out we started seeing bear tracks in the trail. Dismounting, we inspected the tracks of a large grizzly in the snow. They were only a few minutes old. We tied the horses and followed the tracks, expecting to see the bear at any moment. Three hours later all we had seen were tracks. We returned to the horses for lunch.

After a short rest and a moose sandwich, we rode further into the burn. Moose sign was everywhere. We continued slowly through the burn for an hour or so. And then, through the burned trees ahead, startled moose began moving in all directions. Fifteen or more crashed through the brittle downfall. At first we saw only cows and calves, but then a small bull stopped to look back at us. And then a very big bull burst into the open. He also paused and looked over his shoulder in our direction.

Because I knew I could never see a moose to compare with the one I had taken in the Northwest Territories, I hadn't planned to shoot a moose on this trip. But this bull was exceptional. I quickly changed my mind. We were only a half day from base camp. Why not?

A bull too good to pass up, taken in September of 1977.

I jumped off the mare. But the bull was now out of sight—the brush was too high. There were no boulders or stumps close by, only a leaning tree. I scrambled up the slanted snag for a better view. He was still standing there, gazing curiously at our horses, probably trying to decide if these were funny looking cow moose. Though I was weaving and unsteady, the shot dropped him quickly. The other moose crashed off into the distance.

After dressing and packing, we headed back to camp in high spirits, already looking forward to a hot bath and a warm bed. Rick confided that this was the best bull he had guided for in his seven years working here. Later the tape showed him to be fifty-eight inches wide. With twelve points on each side, he scored over two hundred points, well into the Boone and Crockett.

Ron was already in camp but reported nothing shot. He'd seen elk, mule deer, and even a whitetail, but no moose, sheep, or bear.

For the next three days we hunted from base camp. Each morning we rode out together, but then split up to hunt. Ron saw moose every day but no trophies. Rick and I saw animals but no sheep or bears, mostly just lots of horse tracks on the muddy trails . . . too many hunters!

From Dawn Until Dusk

On the fifth day Don flew us to his highest sheep camp. We were to hunt there for the next several days, and then hunt our way the thirty miles back to base camp. Several good bull moose were spotted from the plane, lifting our spirits somewhat.

Landing at sheep camp was an experience in itself. As we descended, no strip was visible, just unbroken timber! We came in low across a small lake toward the cabin. At the last minute we saw a strip, though it was more like a tunnel in the timber than a real airstrip.

With deft precision Don guided the little plane onto the narrow passage, turned, and taxied back to the antler-covered cabin. I congratulated Don on staying alive all these years. He just shrugged, giving me a sour look.

We were at the lower end of a high, glacier-fed drainage, appropriately named "Paradise Valley." The cabin was comfortable, and we soon settled in for the next several days.

Many fine rams had been taken here, and the landscape showed little sign of use by hunters and horses. It seemed as if our chances were improving.

Next morning we had ridden only a mile or so when a small animal ran through an opening just off the trail. "Wolverine!" I jerked my rifle from the boot but had no chance for a shot. There was another glimpse of him bounding through the brush, but then he was gone.

Rick and I progressed up the valley to a low ridge that provided a view of the entire head of the drainage. We settled down on opposite sides of a huge boulder to glass glacial basins around us.

I had learned years before to remove my rifle from the saddle scabbard when I dismounted. Sometimes a horse will decide to roll, forgetting about the saddle on his back—and of course destroying a rifle carelessly left aboard. As I settled to glass, I placed the rifle within reach beside me. I looked the valley over for several minutes, and lowered my glasses to rest. For some reason I looked over my left shoulder and up the rocky slope. There stood an enormous black wolf! He was frozen still as a statue, staring at the horses a hundred yards behind me. So far he hadn't seen me, and Rick was around the boulder, out of sight. I very slowly reached across and moved my rifle into shooting position. I judged him to be about two hundred yards away. I held the crosshairs dead on. He still hadn't moved when I shot, but at the sound of my rifle he jumped high into the air and tumbled out of sight.

Rick and I ran quickly up to where I had last seen him, but he was gone. We hurried down the hill . . . and there he was, running flat out and apparently unhurt. I fired several times but never touched him. We could only sit and watch him cross the broad valley and go up the other side. Through my binoculars I saw him waver and stumble. I told Rick I thought he was hurt. He said for me to not get my hopes up. "Even if he's hit, these things have a lot of stamina. It's unlikely we'll find him."

I continued to watch him closely, though, and soon he stumbled again. Then he lay down for a few seconds. For the next half mile he struggled on, up and then down, and up again. Finally he staggered around a rocky outcropping, into a wide snow field and out of sight. He didn't emerge up the other side.

After several minutes I told Rick I was going after him. He tried to discourage me, saying I would never see him again. I insisted, though, and he grudgingly went along. The snowfield remained in our sight as we crossed the mile and a half to it. The wolf never reappeared. We rounded a corner onto the snowfield, and there he was. And away he went! He had been lying in the snow, apparently to stop the bleeding. He ran now with renewed vigor. But this time he was close, and I dropped him with one shot. Coal black and heavily furred, he was a gorgeous animal—a once in a lifetime trophy and a bonus I never expected.

The first shot had been low in the front of his chest. It had cut a big gash through skin and muscle but had not hit bone. He had simply bled until growing too weak to go on. He likely would have survived had we not quickly followed up. Another lesson in persistence. By the time we had removed the head and beautiful pelt, it was time to head back to camp. On the way back we spotted a huge bull moose in the aspens above us—maybe one for Ron tomorrow.

That night in camp I experienced the spookiest event of my life. We had been asleep an hour or two when I was awakened by the mournful cries of wolves just a few feet from the cabin. They were so close, and the cries so sorrowful, the hair was raised on the back of my neck.

From Dawn Until Dusk

"Ron. Hey Ron, wake up."

"What . . . ?"

"Did you hear that?"

"Yeah . . ." Then he snored.

The wolves again sang their mournful serenade, even closer than before.

Ron bolted upright in his bag. "What the hell was that?"

The music continued for several minutes, and then abruptly quit. The wolves were gone—leaving us shook up, to say the least.

Somehow they had known we had killed a member of their pack, and had carried his remains back to our camp. Maybe they were hoping to find him alive—or maybe they were paying their last respects. At any rate the event left quite an impression.

Our time was now getting short, and Ron was getting a little nervous. Next morning he headed up to where we had seen the moose while Rick and I hunted downriver looking for caribou or bear. As luck would have it, we spotted a huge bull moose with several cows, and we watched him for most of the morning. We returned to camp, hoping that if Ron hadn't found the other bull, they would return early enough to go after this one. We did some cleaning and cooking, and planned our hunt for the next day. We would go after some goats we could see on the cliffs across the lake.

Ron did come in early, and he had an unusual trophy and a tall tale. They had spotted a bull early and had gone right after him. The brush was thick, however, and they had lost sight of him as they got close. But soon Ron spotted him staring down at them from two hundred yards up the mountain. With the bull looking directly at him, all he could see was face and antlers. He had no opportunity for a rest and so fired offhand—sighting right between the eyes. The bull collapsed and rolled over out of sight. Ron and his guide struggled through the brush up the steep hillside, and soon found where the bull had fallen—but there was no bull. They searched in widening circles. No blood nor any sign of a hit. As they stopped and scratched their heads, Ron spotted a bull stepping into the open a few hundred feet below them.

"There he is!"

"No, that's not him—he only has one antler."

They looked at each other, and hurried back up to where the

Wary and intelligent, wolves are a prized trophy in the North.

bull had first fallen. Yep, there it was, hanging up high in the brush, the other antler—shot off just above the base. The antler was a beauty, and if the other was its equal he would have gone high in the book. Ron thought it was a great joke and had no regrets after losing his trophy. "Sometimes you get the bull, sometimes you don't."

Next morning we were up early for goats. Rick and I had a long, hard climb ahead of us. We threw the frosty saddles on the groaning horses, rode across the river, and stayed in the saddle as far as possible up the steep mountainside. From there we went on foot. After two hours climbing from ledge to ledge through thick, intertwined brush, we rounded a hump and spotted a goat ahead. He'd seen us, and was already working his way around the cliff. As he moved, several others appeared, staring down at us from various perches on the cliff face.

Which of these were billies? And of the billies, which was the biggest? All looked big, all had thick, white coats, and all had horns. One of the bigger ones, however, had a coat that was somewhat yellowed, and his horns stood out, long and shiny black. Without further hesitation I aimed and fired. Big mistake!

From Dawn Until Dusk

He was directly above us and down he came. As he gained momentum, rocks broke loose and joined him in his downhill plummet. We had only a few seconds to recognize the danger and dive behind a huge boulder.

Debris passed over and around us. When the avalanche stilled, we poked out our heads, looking for the goat. He was just a few yards up the slope, hung on a twisted snag. A very lucky break. If he had gone past us he would have fallen several hundred feet straight down. After quickly skinning him, we retraced our path back to the horses. Ron and his guide were already there. They also had a beautiful goat—his first trophy of the hunt. We happily rode back to camp and spent the rest of the day caring for our skins.

Hunting had been good and we had shot several animals, but still we had not seen what we had come for. No bears and no sheep, and our time was about up. That evening we had some serious conversation with our guides, and decided to start packing back toward base camp. We would try hunting a mountain that had never failed to yield sheep.

The next morning found us on a snow-covered trail beside the Sikanni Chief River. I rode single file behind Rick. When I spotted a huge grizzly just across the river, I jumped off my horse, announcing, "Bear!" Ron and both guides had also seen him and jumped off just as quickly, but then our rifle scopes transformed the silver-tipped bear into a silver-tipped boulder. We rode on sheepishly until we reached the base of a large, grass-covered mountain. This was the spot.

Glassing revealed a small band of rams near the top, but from this distance we couldn't tell how big they were—only that they were rams. We decided to split up, with Ron hunting on one side of the sheep and me on the other. The climb was tough but not dangerous. When we were within five hundred yards, the rams got to their feet and slowly moved off. We saw that all were three-quarter curl or less, none legal. Ron and Shane returned, and said the rams had run right past them. After all this time we had finally found rams, only to be disappointed again. Such is hunting.

Now we were tired enough to start thinking of home again. Dusk was already upon us as we rode into the grassy meadow where we planned to camp. Just as we cleared the trees, a big bull moose broke from cover and ran toward the other side of the clearing. Ron baled off and ran across and into the trees after him. Soon a shot echoed across the valley. We rode across to find Ron standing over a dandy bull. He was all smiles.

At dawn we were on the trail again, packhorses loaded with meat and trophies. Day after tomorrow we would be on the jet headed home—and we were ready.

But there was one more adventure in store for us. At ten o'clock that morning, we saw movement on a high ridge above us. Caribou! We tied the horses, split up, and climbed the mountain. By the time we reached the ridge, I was exhausted all over again. After a very short rest, we began to sidehill basin to basin. Finally we found the caribou bedded in a tight group. They jumped up, and the only good bull stayed surrounded by cows. As they fled over the mountaintop. Rick said, "Just wait, they'll be back." We sat down, and sure enough here they came for another look. This time they were strung out—and I snapped a shot as they ran past. The bull stumbled, fell, and slid down the mountain in the deep snow. He came to rest a half mile below us.

Now I had all the trophies except for the ones I had come for. I had mixed feelings, and could not help being a little disappointed.

After retrieving the horses and packing my caribou, we waited for Ron. Finally we saw them coming, also packing a caribou—nearly identical to mine.

We had a Spartan camp that night, but were back in base camp before noon the next day.

As we flew out we discussed our feelings about the hunt. Our guides had confided that Don's sheep hunting statistics were a little misleading. Don only took five sheep hunters a year, and almost without fail his first two hunters bagged rams. Sometimes the third hunter did, but almost never the last two. We were the last two in 1977. But we finally decided that the beauty of this game-rich country had been worth the cost of the hunt, and the animals we had found were just a bonus. Our quest had been for sheep and griz—but now we would just have to return to British Columbia for another try.

Allen killed his first deer, left, at the age of twelve. His brother, Mark, killed his first elk, above, two hours later and a quarter mile away.

Chapter 12

A Buck and a Bull for the Boys

In 1982 our family moved to Montana for good. Since first coming west in 1966, we had returned for summer vacations, but except for one year when my son Mark was fourteen, the boys had not been on a Montana hunt. Neither Mark nor Allen had hunted elk, and Allen, only twelve, had not yet taken a deer.

We all eagerly looked forward to our first hunting season together in Montana. Mark wanted to shoot an elk in the worst way, and Allen just wanted a deer with "big horns."

The season opened in late October with bluebird weather—and game predictably hard to find. Weekends found us out early and home late. With the exception of a few blue grouse, we had no meat for the pot.

By mid-November Allen was getting discouraged and wanted to sleep late on the weekend. Mark remained undaunted and optimistic. Then the snow came. Thursday morning we awoke to eight inches of fluffy white stuff in town—and it was still coming down. Saturday should be perfect. By Friday afternoon the sky had cleared and the bitter cold had moved in, but the beautiful, bright blue sky made the temperature bearable.

On Saturday morning we were high on the mountain by

From Dawn Until Dusk

Crystal Cross Rock in Tom Minor basin. Our friend, Max, who owned the land, had suggested that this place was a good spot for elk, and a real sleeper for big mule deer. The mountainside where we had parked was open except for tall sage and huge boulders, with pockets of juniper and fir. Max had instructed us to park, climb over the top, and hunt the timber edge at first light.

When we stepped from the truck the bitter cold made us all want to jump back into the warmth. Little Allen declared that by gum he was gonna stay right where he was. I didn't blame him. "Okay, but don't leave the engine running. Just start it occasionally to warm up."

Mark and I headed off through the deep snow with assurances to Allen that we would be back in a couple hours. We had gone only a few hundred yards when we spotted several mule deer does and a forkhorn buck on a low point below the truck. The light was still dim, but through the binoculars I confirmed that the buck was too small to interest us. But there must be a bigger buck somewhere. Swinging the binoculars I searched through the pockets of brush and rocks carefully—and yep, there he was! A very nice four-by-four lying in a tiny, snow-filled basin five hundred yards above the truck.

We thought of Allen. Mark volunteered to go get him while I stayed behind and kept an eye on the buck.

After rousting Allen from his snug nest, they both slipped around and bellied up to a low, windswept ridge across from the buck. He lay still unaware of us—but they couldn't see him! They looked up at me, and I signalled that he was still right there. After moving to the side a few yards they finally spotted him. Allen slipped up to a big rock to take a rest. I waited for the shot but none came. I could see Mark growing restless as Allen scurried over to another rock for a better view.

Finally he settled down. The crack of the 6 mm echoed back. The buck simply slumped in his bed. A clean kill at over 150 yards—not bad for a little kid! After photos, field dressing, and loading, we jumped in the truck to warm up.

Allen wanted to head back to town to show off his buck, but Mark and I hadn't hunted at all—and it was a perfect day. We debated while we toasted in the cab.

"Well, while we are deciding what to do, let's just drive around a little."

"Sounds good."

The snow squealed under the tires as we crept up the steep logging road. After only a quarter mile or so, and with the banks nearly vertical above and below the road, Mark hissed, "Elk." He was staring up the mountain. I couldn't see from my side, so I baled out. Sure enough, several elk were filing out from the timber just above us. So far they were all cows. They passed through a narrow opening in the timber before disappearing again.

Mark came around to my side. I told him to take a rest off the hood. "Get ready. A bull is going to slip through after those cows and you'll only have a second to shoot."

Sure enough, after a long procession of cows and calves, antlers appeared—and Mark's rifle cracked. Elk ran in all directions, but the bull had disappeared. Had Mark hit him? We struggled up through the knee-deep snow to where he had been standing. And there he lay, a big five point dropped in his tracks. Mark was thrilled beyond description. Just to think, we had almost quit and gone home. Now we had both a buck and a bull for the boys to show off.

The elk had fallen directly above the truck. After more photos and field dressing, we began pulling him down through a tangle of sagebrush. We hadn't gone far, though, when the bull gained momentum and began to move on its own. It ran over me, ripping my clothes and pummeling me against the rocks. By the time we got the bull to the road, Mark and I were both scratched and bruised. We decided elk were dangerous animals—especially when dead.

Now that he was on the road it should have been a simple matter to get him loaded. Wrong! The three of us were able to get the head and neck up over the tailgate—but no further. No matter how hard we tried we just couldn't get him loaded. What to do now?

After some deliberation I got a length of rope from the cab and tied the bull's head up on the tailgate. I told the boys to load up.

"You're not going to drag him?"

From Dawn Until Dusk

"Yep, it's only forty miles home. By the time we get there he won't weigh so much."

Mark half believed me, and was pretty upset as I dragged his bull down the snow covered road. But I was remembering the little side road where we had parked earlier. After retracing our path to the parking spot, I simply dragged the bull up onto the uphill road, untied him, slid him to the edge, pulled around and below him, backed up, and slid him in. No problem!

This had been a morning to remember, father and sons together on a frigid mountain in Montana. For a dad it just doesn't get any better.

Chapter 13

Mark the Hunter

As dusk settled into dark, snow fluttered down from the leaden sky. Before long the grass was bent flat and covered with a white blanket. We knew that the morning would bring excellent hunting conditions, so Mark and I snuggled into our down bags with anticipation. Morning would come too quickly, and it was oh so cold. But the bulls were up there in the mountains, which meant we needed to be there as well.

An hour before sunrise, our bare feet stuck to a frost-covered floor. We quickly pulled on our wool socks, then long johns and heavy boots. The temperature had plunged to well below zero, and a breeze rattled at the icicles above the door.

Mark dressed quickly and started a fire. As the terrible cold abated, we ate a quick breakfast in relative comfort. Outside, however, the frigid wind was taking the fresh snow and piling it up into thick drifts.

We slipped into the cab of my old Ford pickup. The engine groaned and slowly turned, then miraculously started. As we sat in the dark letting the engine warm, we discussed our strategy. We wouldn't be able to hunt on foot under these conditions, so a drive up the mountain looked like our best shot.

From Dawn Until Dusk

Tires shrieked on snow as we crept up a logging road toward the high pastures. We were in no hurry now. The cab was warm and elk could be anywhere around us.

We drove from the heavy timber into an open basin. The sky had lightened enough for us to see the dark shapes of trees against snow. We parked, and sat waiting for the light to get better. We talked about other hunts and other cold mornings. The time passed easily.

After a few minutes we idled forward through the blowing snow. We soon spotted a small herd of elk across a basin on an open hillside. Cows and calves. But then out from the trees stepped a spike bull, and then two more. The herd began to string out across the meadow, moving toward a second patch of timber. It wasn't long before they had all disappeared. Mark and I glanced at each other, grinning. We hadn't even considered trying for them; sometimes it is best to simply enjoy the moment.

We drove forward, navigating switchbacks, growling up the steep incline, finally reaching the top of the ridge where we had planned to park. We got out of the truck and began to hunt on foot around the slope ahead. The snow blew so hard that crystals stung our exposed skin, nearly blinding us. I said, "Maybe we should drive around just a little farther."

Back in the truck, we again idled slowly on the old road, watching a blizzard swirl past our windshield.

"There, did you see that?" Mark asked.

"What?"

"A cow and a calf just crossed the road down at the curve."

"Mark, why don't you ease down there to see what's going on?"

I sat in the truck and watched as Mark quietly moved through the drifting snow. When he was nearly out of sight, he stopped in mid stride, then sank into weeds by the roadside. He'd clearly seen something. Soon I saw them too, a cow and calf walking toward us—then another cow, then another. Though we had licenses for cows as well as bulls, I knew Mark wanted a big bull. They stepped off the road and into the trees, still unaware of us.

Mark rose from his hiding place and moved forward again, gun ready. After he moved out of sight around the curve, I quietly opened and closed the truck door, then began following his tracks before they could disappear.

I soon saw where he had left the logging road and moved up the steep hillside into heavy brush. At that moment, I heard a muffled shot from above.

Moving faster now, I circled through the dense brush, hoping to catch a glimpse of the action. Two mule deer does came bouncing out past me, but all else was quiet.

The wind carried my whistle away. I heard no answer. I continued up toward where I had heard the shot. I crossed the single track of a big bull going up in the same direction, then the tracks of several cows. I whistled again, and again there was no answer. Being a dad, I began to worry just a little. Maybe he had fallen and shot himself. But no, I knew Mark better than that. He was fine.

I went back to the road and started following his trail from the beginning. It soon went through a lodgepole thicket, nearly lost in a jumble of elk sign. He'd been running after them. No wonder I couldn't sort it out.

I saw the track of a large bull among the smaller prints of cows and calves. Mark had shot at a bull then, and since I could see no blood, he had probably missed.

Mark's trail crossed an open park, then went back into the timber. He was still running, hoping to catch them in one of the openings. But in his hurry I saw where he'd made a mistake. The bull had split off and angled down the hill into a twisted mass of downed timber. Mark had missed seeing that one track leaving the rest.

I decided to follow the bull to be sure he wasn't wounded. I slowed down almost to a stop, eyes searching the dark jungle ahead. My steps were muffled in the deep snow, and the wind carried my scent away and up the mountain.

A few hundred feet into the tangle, a great bull rose ghostlike from the swirling curtain of snow. He lifted his nose and turned, stumbling over a steep bank out of sight. He was badly hurt, and I could hear him fall in the dead branches below. I ran toward him, but he was already on his feet again, stumbling through the densest thicket imaginable.

From Dawn Until Dusk

Although he was out of sight, I could see where he would soon be passing through a small opening. I brought the rifle to my shoulder and waited. There was movement, then a faint outline through a screen of falling snow. He looked back at me. I could only see his massive antlers. Again he began to run. I fired at his fleeting image and saw my bullet chip a four-inch fir tree just in front of my barrel.

The bull ran through the timber below, too far away for a shot. But as he moved into more open forest, he stumble and fell again. This time he stayed down. As quickly as possible I moved toward him. When he heard me coming, he struggled to his feet, then fell again, sliding and wedging his body against a tree just above the logging road. I quickly ended his misery.

I expected Mark to be coming along soon, gravitating toward my shots. In the meantime I decided to field dress this magnificent creature by myself. After some serious grunting, however, I saw that there was no way I would be able to budge him from his spot against the tree.

I headed off back toward the truck, still looking for Mark. I hoped he might be there waiting for me. Instead I found a note on a scrap of paper written with the lead tip of a bullet.

"Shot at a big bull running through the timber. May have missed but have gone back to trail him again—just to be sure. Will see you later. Love, Mark."

Mark just could not give up on a bull that might be hurt. My problem was still not solved, however. I needed help, and Mark was off and running over the mountain again. I decided to drive around below the bull and wait for Mark to show up.

As I positioned the truck below the elk, I saw a flash of orange far up the mountainside. I blew the horn. Through my binoculars, Mark stopped and waved. He was soon beside the truck with a big smile and a question on his face. "What did you shoot at? Did you kill the bull?"

"I finished him off, but he's your bull."

"I thought I must of hit him. He was so close, but elk were running everywhere! I'm so glad you found him. Thanks, Dad."

Mark and I examined his trophy. Apart from my mercy shot,

there was only a single bullet hole, just a little far back but a good hit under the circumstances. The stamina of this great animal had been extraordinary.

Extracting him from his resting place was all the two of us could handle, but eventually we had him dressed—then easily slid him down and into the truck bed.

The snow was still blowing, the sky was gray, and the temperature was still below zero—but with a bull elk in the truck everything seemed warm and bright. We knew that there would be bucks and bulls to hunt in days to come, and there would be other frigid mornings warmed by the love and companionship that all fathers and sons should know.

Chapter 14

An Unexpected Blizzard

September in Montana can be like October in most of the rest of the country. The afternoons are warm and pleasant but the mornings are often frosty. Still, none of us expected the blizzard that blew in on September 18, 1983.

Soon after moving to Montana in 1982, Eunice and I bought property south of Livingston. We were going to build the art gallery of which we had long dreamed. Before we could begin construction, however, I became friends with a local taxidermist, and our original gallery plan was expanded to include a larger building that would house not only the gallery but a museum of North American wildlife as well.

Construction of our building progressed on schedule, but the taxidermy fell behind. It became obvious the museum would have to come later. In the meantime we needed to fill the space with a tenant.

There were three sporting goods stores downtown, and the most active of these obviously needed more space. I approached one of the partners with a proposition. Within three days I had a tenant. Wilderness Outfitters and the Burl Jones Roche Jaune

Galerie became neighbors, and would remain side by side for fifteen years.

One of the partners was Mark B., who had recently been licensed as a big game outfitter. He had also acquired a one-hundred-thousand acre hunting lease in the Belt Mountains west of White Sulfur Springs. But because the deal had only recently been finalized, he had no hunters for the upcoming fall. He volunteered to guide both my sons, Mark and Allen, bowhunting for elk.

This was a great opportunity for the boys, neither of whom had bagged a bull with archery equipment—and Allen had never shot one at all.

Mark B. had been doing some scouting, and had us revved up with reports of the many big bulls he'd seen. The hunts would be on weekends after the rut was underway. Allen would be the first hunter. He was so excited from mid-August on that he could hardly sleep.

On a Friday in September, Mark asked me if Allen could hunt the following day. Of course I said yes, and we agreed to meet in time to get into the hunt area before dawn.

Saturday morning dawned frosty and clear, with the promise of another glorious "big sky" day. We arrived on the hunting lease just as the sky turned golden in the east. Mark was using one of the original ranch buildings as his hunting camp, and we planned to spend the night there, keeping the mice and pack rats company. Pulling into the fenced yard, mule deer bounded away in all directions. As we unloaded our gear, a bugle echoed from the mountain above.

Mark wanted to spend the morning scouting. Once we had the elk located, we would plan an attack for the afternoon.

In his big crew cab truck we growled up the mountainside, touring from one park to another. The mountain was covered with dense stands of lodgepole pine and fir, interrupted by small grassy parks. Perfect elk habitat. We saw sign everywhere, including heavily-traveled trails, beds and wallows in the damp bottoms, and thick pine saplings shredded by rutting bulls.

Our first sighting was of a small group of cows and calves running through a little park ahead, followed by a gigantic six point bull. Allen and I sat stunned behind our binoculars. We

From Dawn Until Dusk

weren't sure we'd ever seen a bigger bull, even in Yellowstone Park. We looked at each other with silly grins.

We drove up onto a long ridge that overlooked a wide, heavily-timbered valley. We left the vehicle to walk further up the ridge, glassing and listening. Bugles, grunts, and donkey-like braying arose from the timber below. We couldn't see any elk, but it was obvious this was a real hotspot. We now knew where we would be hunting in the evening. Mark appeared to be very calm and confident but Allen was a nervous wreck.

Allen had never fired an arrow at a living thing, although he had practiced with his new compound bow until he could place every arrow into the kill zone at up to thirty yards. He had confided in me that he wanted a shot at fifteen yards or less. He was just too unsure to take a shot any further, and simply did not want to chance wounding one of these magnificent animals.

After a nice lunch provided by Mark, we lounged in the warm sun on the camp porch, napping to catch up on the sleep missed the night before. It was a beautiful afternoon, with no hint of the changes brewing to the north and west.

With two hours of daylight remaining, we again loaded up in Mark's truck and drove to the bottom of the mountain. While Mark and Allen readied their gear, I glassed the open slopes behind us. I noted that the long ridge we were on actually led down into the open country in line with Mark's camp three or four miles away. I also noted a long fence separating pastures. It ran in a north and south direction, with north being somewhat west of the town of White Sulfur Springs some twelve miles away.

As we left the truck and drifted up the ridge into the timber, the sky grew overcast and the temperature began to drop. This didn't bother us at all. In fact it made us even more excited. A weather change could stimulate the rutting bulls to even greater activity.

Within seconds of leaving the truck we heard the first bugle, followed immediately by another. Soon we were hearing the same cacophony of sounds we had heard that morning. All the bull elk in the Belt Mountains were here, and singing their lungs out.

As luck would have it, the most frantic bull was also the closest. We moved down to the edge of a small park a few hundred yards above the bugle. Mark moved back about forty feet to hide behind a juniper bush. Allen positioned himself behind some small firs.

By now a few flakes of snow were falling, and the temperature had dropped nearly thirty degrees since noon. The wind sighed through the trees. But visibility was still good, and the fresh wind carried our scent up and away from the elk below us. A perfect setup! Now all we needed was a love-stricken bull to complete the picture.

Mark bugled and grunted. I was impressed with his calling ability. His call sounded like the real thing. The amorous bull in the timber below responded immediately, and when Mark called again, it sounded like the elk was coming our way. Mark whispered to Allen, "Get ready. He's coming fast." Within minutes the bull was approaching through the trees, grunting and coughing at every step. His belly jerked and quivered, and his uh-uh-uh-uhs reverberated from an extended throat. He stopped at about one hundred yards out and whistled a long, shrill call. He seemed confused by not being able to see his challenger, and started to turn back. Mark broke off a limb and raked it in the brush.

The change was electric. The bull charged up the hill toward us. This time he did not hesitate, running toward Mark and passing directly in front of Allen—at a range of ten yards or so. Mark grunted softly, and the bull stopped, head up, staring at the empty space where the other bull should be . . . and Allen's arrow struck him perfectly behind the shoulder. The bull bolted forward, made three jumps down the mountain, and fell forward on his nose, dead.

Mark and I both erupted from our nests and danced with joy around Allen, who was still recovering from the shock of what he had just accomplished. He had actually bagged a trophy bull elk with his bow at fourteen years old.

None of us would forget this thrilling moment. And now Mark had reference photos to help sell his hunts for the next year.

During all the excitement, none of us had noticed that the snow and wind were getting serious. By the time photos were complete the ground was covered with a heavy blanket. Dusk was coming on fast.

Mark recognized a potential problem and volunteered to hike back off the mountain to get the truck. In the meantime, Allen and I would dress the elk. As the snow was now getting quite heavy and the wind creating a real blizzard, I was uncertain. I felt that all of us should quickly gut the elk and then get off the mountain together, coming back tomorrow to retrieve our animal.

But Mark insisted that he would be back by the time we had the elk ready to travel. We wouldn't find it necessary to come back in the morning. Before we could debate further, he was off toward the truck.

Allen and I had the elk field dressed within minutes, and then anxiously began to wait for Mark to return. The snow piled up, collecting in drifts. I began to seriously doubt that Mark would be able to come up with the truck, much less find us in the dark and in a blizzard. Before it became totally dark, we gathered some wood and tried to get a fire started, but the wind and dampness made it impossible. We were getting wet, and by now the temperature was well below freezing.

Two hours had passed since Mark had left us, and it was obvious he was either stuck or couldn't find his way back to us. We would have to save ourselves or freeze to death on this snow-covered mountain.

Allen was a bit panicky, but I calmed him with assurances that if we stayed confident we could make it off the mountain. I wasn't so sure myself, but he needed to be reassured.

I instructed him to stay very close behind me. The worst thing would be for us to become separated. Visibility was zero, so we had to be very careful not to fall or run into a sharp limb.

I told him what I had observed earlier. The ridge above us sloped gradually down into the prairie below, in a direct line with Mark's camp. Once we were on the flats we would be able to follow the fence, if we could find it.

In drifts that were now up to our knees, we struggled up to the ridge top, then swung downhill. Once in the open, the wind became even more fierce, but it was blowing steadily from the northwest, and helped us maintain our orientation down the open slope.

After what seemed like hours, we were off the mountain and had soon found the fence. With lifted spirits, we sang old John Denver songs and waded through the ever-deepening snow. I

Allen's first bull elk was taken with a bow when Allen was only fourteen years old.

---

assured Allen we would eventually hit a road that would lead us into town—even if we missed Mark's house.

As we struggled through an especially deep drift, Allen tripped over a coil of discarded barbed wire. He regained his feet, but as he brushed off his freezing face he realized his glasses were missing. Frantically we searched the deep snow, but soon gave up and continued our journey. Glasses could be replaced but we had to keep moving to keep warm and survive.

Following the fence was easy, and we were feeling pretty good about what we had accomplished so far. And then through the swirling blizzard I thought I saw an airport light swing across on the horizon. We stopped to reassess. I knew there was a small airport near town, but there was no way we could be close

From Dawn Until Dusk

enough to see its light. Then the beam swung across in the other direction. It had to be Mark. He was being smart and providing a beacon for us.

We changed directions, leaving the fence in favor of heading toward the light. As we hustled over the low hill, we saw the light again. This time we were sure it was a vehicle. It was moving across in front of us. We sprinted across the level plain on a path to intercept Mark. Just as we were about to give up the chase, Mark again swung around—this time illuminating us in his headlights.

The warm cab felt like heaven, and we were pretty well recovered by the time we made it back to the cabin. With very little discussion about our ordeal, we had a nice dinner; and after changing into dry clothes, relaxed by the fire before turning in.

From our beds, Allen and I talked long into the night about our adventure and how thankful we were to be here and not out on that mountain freezing to death.

The next morning, with all four tires chained up, we again ground our way up the long ridge. Mark unerringly drove to within a few feet of the elk. After quickly loading the bull, we were off the mountain and on our way home.

A great adventure for me, and an unforgettable event for Allen. Our story could have ended with headlines in the Livingston *Enterprise*, but instead there was little mention of our near disaster except to family and close friends. For weeks Allen and I exchanged knowing smiles and an occasional hug.

Chapter 15

Another Elk for Allen

I whispered, "Ron look over there. Right there in the small park below those aspens. Three, four, five . . . Look at those two at the top—they're almost white. They have to be bulls."

The elk were more than two miles away, and the evening was growing late, but we still had tomorrow to hunt. Now we knew where to be at first light.

In the mid eighties, I traded a bronze to a rancher in the Castle Mountains of Central Montana, gaining access to the hunting on his property. My good friend Ron had found two days between business trips to come along on a hunt. During the September bow season, Euni, the boys, and I had located over a dozen bull elk and a couple dozen mule deer and whitetail bucks on this same ranch.

The first day of Ron's hunt found us concentrating on mule deer, and he had shot a beautiful mule deer buck just at daylight. The rest of the day we cruised the logging roads looking for elk. We had no luck until we saw the two bulls just before dark across a broad valley.

The next morning we crept to the edge of a high mountain pasture. The eastern sky turned from lead gray to gold while a

From Dawn Until Dusk

light snow fell in the basins further up. We were going to get more snow, and a lot of it. But for now the ground was clear and dry, and the elk were . . . gone!

I had been certain we would find them right where they'd been feeding the evening before, but they had disappeared. We hunted on foot around the mountainside, glassing, but saw not a single elk. Finally Ron had to leave for his appointments.

Back in Livingston, I settled down with the family for the evening. "Well Allen, what do you think?"

"Tomorrow's Saturday, and we know the elk are up there somewhere."

"You want to try and catch them early—say leave here around five?"

"Maybe we should sleep in, hunt in the evening. What do you think?"

I was tired and welcomed a good night's sleep. There would still be Sunday morning if we failed to find a bull on the evening hunt.

By about noon Allen and I were on our way back to the Castles. As I drove I tapped the steering wheel in time to the Nitty Gritty Dirt Band. By two we had reached camp, unloaded groceries, and headed back up the mountain on foot. We were going to start by hunting the parks and aspen groves on the lower ridges. If Allen eased along the top of the open parks while I slipped through the thickets further down, I hoped that I would push something up to him.

We parted, and within thirty minutes I was into elk. Passing through a large thicket of stunted fir and pine, I had just come to the edge of a semi-open stand of aspen when I saw a cow grazing fifty feet ahead. She threw her head up as another elk called from further up in the aspens. Elk were soon mewing and calling all around me.

This wasn't helping Allen at all. How could I push them up to him?

Before I could make a plan, one cow drifted downwind. It froze for an instant, then crashed off down the mountain. Wrong way! The other elk began drifting away. Then I heard a clash of antlers directly above me. Two bulls were fighting, and they were close to where Allen was supposed to be.

I slipped quietly toward the sound. Suddenly everything became silent. I froze, and as I stared through the white aspen trunks, a tawny hide passed for an instant before my eyes.

"Bang!"

Several seconds passed with no other sound. He must have got him!

"Bang!"

Just the right interval for the finisher. I was sure he had one now.

"Bang!"

Uh-oh, he was getting away!

"Bang!"

He'd missed for sure.

Slowly I moved up through the deep grass among the aspens toward the sound of the shots. I half expected to see a crippled elk come through the trees toward me, and was on high alert to fire my rifle if necessary. My heart stopped when the brush cracked just ahead, and a doe bounded out past me.

I gathered my wits and again walked toward Allen.

My whistled signal brought no answer. I yelled out his name.

"Here I am."

Just up the hill at the edge of an aspen grove, Allen was kneeling over something—I could see an antler!

As I approached, Allen stood up with a smile from ear to ear. "I got him, Dad. And he's a dandy!"

Sure enough, a big raghorn bull lay at Allen's feet. As we began the field dressing, Allen told me the details of his kill.

Shortly after we separated, he had spotted a lone cow elk in the middle of this open field, licking a mineral deposit. As he had crept to a good vantage point, she lay down in the field, but his movement spooked several other elk bedded nearby in the scattered trees. They ran off into dark timber. He searched for antlers, and glimpsed a big rack through his binoculars just as the animal disappeared into the shadows.

With nothing to lose, he decided to follow them into the thick stuff to see if he could spot the bull again. These were a totally separate group of animals from what I had seen, and Allen had not heard the bulls fighting above me.

Soon after entering the lodgepole thicket he could see elk

From Dawn Until Dusk

moving ahead of him. He inched forward on his belly, seeing only legs with occasionally a tan side or an ear and eye. As he crept closer, one elk moved toward him without sound, and lowered its head, trying to see what sort of creature was in there with them. It had antlers, big ones. It moved out of sight again.

With his rifle ready Allen continued forward. There. There he was again, moving into the open! No, not the same one—a smaller bull, a raghorn with a crazy antler on one side.

Before we left camp, Allen and I had talked about what he would shoot. "Will you be happy with a spike," I asked. "Or are you going to hold out for a big bull?"

"I'll make the decision when I see him, I just don't know."

Well now it was decision time, and with about two seconds of deliberation he sighted through his scope and fired. Immediately he chambered another round, but the elk had dropped out of sight in the tall grass. No sooner had Allen decided the bull was down for good than the animal was up again and running through the trees. Allen fired again, and again the bull dropped, only to rise once more and struggle off. Allen ran to catch up, and as the elk emerged again into another opening he fired the third time. This time the bull dropped for keeps.

By now Allen's adrenaline level was so high that when the bull moved just slightly, Allen made sure with one last round.

In just a few short years of hunting, Allen had bagged more big game than most hunters see in their lifetime. In his first year in Montana he had taken a good four point mule deer north of Yellowstone Park and a heavily-furred black bear in the Crazy Mountains. The following few years brought him a bull elk with his bow, a record-class cougar, two trophy-class pronghorns, and other assorted big game.

Chapter 16

Mountain Lions in Montana

Our day started long before dawn in the frigid mountains of the Absaroka-Beartooth range south of Livingston, Montana. Snow fell softly as we drove up the Mill Creek drainage.

In late winter, mountain lions tend to drift down into the foothills and valleys, following mule deer, their primary food source. With each fresh fall of snow, they leave new tracks, and thus became vulnerable to hunters with well-trained hounds.

This morning Allen I were going to be trailing the big cats with a locally-famous hunter, "Cougar Lee" Fatourus. Lee had been a government hunter in Idaho before moving to Montana several years before. He claimed to have killed more lions than any other man alive. Lee lived in one of the last homes up Mill Creek, and kept a pack of superb hounds.

Mill Creek is a roaring mountain torrent in the spring, but in the winter its voice is muffled by a thick covering of ice and snow. The road wound up a very narrow canyon, following the twists and turns of the stream. The mountainsides rose steeply on both sides, angling toward their summits over ten thousand feet above us.

From Dawn Until Dusk

Allen and I met Lee in his driveway, his hounds barking from their kennels. After a few words, we loaded the dogs into his truck and started up the road, looking for tracks.

We soon got lucky. After only a mile or so, we saw where a big male lion had crossed our path. He had gone straight up the steep mountainside to the east.

We began our hunt with the hounds on leashes. Their excited baying soon convinced Lee that the cat was not far ahead. He released his dogs.

After only a few minutes they were out of hearing far up the nearly vertical mountain. We followed their tracks as rapidly as we could, but the going was slow as the lion passed through tumbled boulders and brush covered with over a foot of snow.

After what seemed like hours of climbing, we heard the hounds far above us. Lee declared they had the cat up a tree.

Eventually we were close enough to hear the whimpers and scratching of toenails on tree bark. Obviously the cat could hear us as well, because the tone of the hounds' barking suddenly changed. Back down the mountain they went. Even though the cat had bailed out of the tree before we had a chance to get close, we weren't too disappointed. He now was headed downhill, directly toward Lee's truck.

Going down went much faster. Soon we approached the dogs barking treed again—but again the big cat jumped out before we could see him. He headed back up the mountain.

Again we followed, slower than before. As we approached tree line for the second time, it became apparent that the lion and the dogs had crossed over the summit. Up that high, the snow would be far too deep for us to follow.

It seemed to me that Lee had surely lost his prize hounds, but he reassured us that we would find them again. They carried radio transmitters on their collars. He had the receiver in his truck.

By the time we struggled off the mountain a second time we were all exhausted. In deep snow and over very rough terrain, we had twice climbed from five thousand to nine thousand feet. But until Lee found his dogs, we were obliged to keep going.

Back at the truck, Lee turned on his radio receiver and began driving up the East Fork of Mill Creek, around the other side of the mountain we had just left. As we approached a vertical side drainage, his receiver began to beep. He pulled off the side of the road. The receiver told him in which direction the dogs had gone, but not how far up they were—and it was a very long way to the top. I prayed they were close, and I'm sure Allen and Lee had the same feeling.

We climbed through deep snow, and climbed, and climbed. As we neared the timberline again we could at last begin to hear the hounds barking treed.

Allen, who was only fourteen years old, was still going strong as we approached the twisted snag on the steep rocky slope, but Lee and I were both in agony. Our leg muscles cramped as we inched our way up the last few yards to our quarry.

The huge cat stared down at us from his perch in a stunted juniper snag. The tree was so small it seemed we could almost touch him. He looked quite bored with the whole situation. He yawned and closed his eyes as if to nap.

After taking a few photos of the cat in the tree, Lee gave Allen the signal to shoot. Allen had carried his .22 magnum rifle three trips up this mountain, and was now happy to put it to use.

On the shot, the lion fell from the tree and slid, snarling and scratching, down the steep, snow-covered slope. He finally came to rest below us. As Allen hurried down, the big cat revived, snarling up at him, face to face.

With the second shot he lay quiet, and we all breathed a sigh of relief.

From here it was all downhill. In the gathering darkness we happily dragged our trophy over the snow to the valley far below. It had taken over twelve hours and three trips to tree line for Allen to take his lion.

Some will say that shooting a lion from a tree is unsportsmanlike. To them I say you haven't been there and you simply do not understand. A lion hunt can be easy but for us it was a test of endurance and determination. Allen's big lion is a trophy to be proud of—and a memory etched forever in our minds.

Our Saturday a few weeks later was booked. The Jones family had planned a day of skiing at Bridger Bowl, north of Bozeman, Montana. Given the several inches of fresh powder that had fallen overnight, conditions would be perfect.

From Dawn Until Dusk

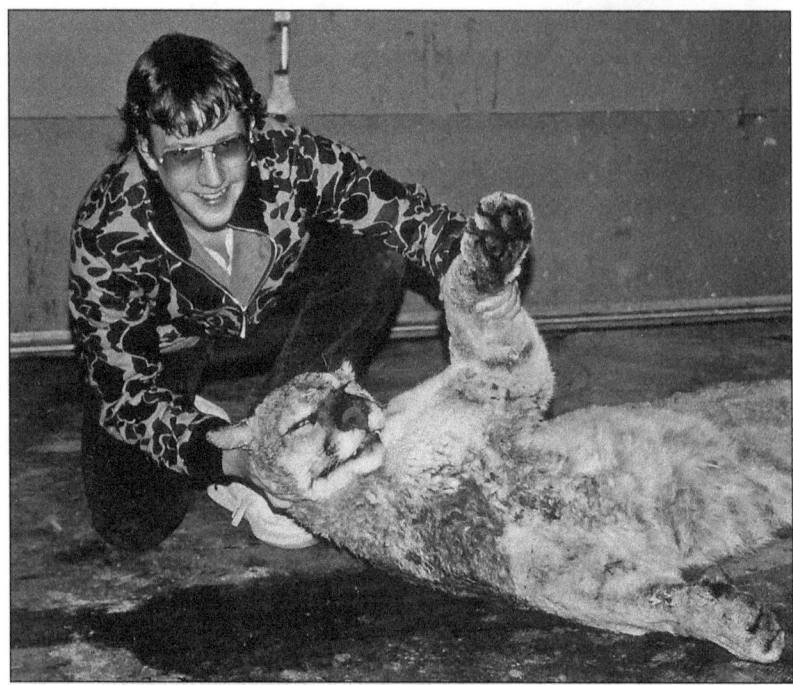

*Allen's big male mountain lion weighed
almost 140 pounds.*

Mark, Allen, Eunice, and I had just completed our second run of the morning and were in the lodge with hot chocolate when a voice over the PA system announced, "Phone call for Burl Jones." One always expects bad news in such a situation, and with apprehension I went to find a phone. But soon I returned to announce that the call was from Lee Fatourus. He had found us through our gallery in Livingston. Lee and I had talked earlier about lion hunting on a likely weekend, and he had agreed to call when he struck a fresh track. Early that morning he had crossed some smoking-hot sign far up in the head of the West Fork of Mill Creek. Mark and I quickly decided skiing could wait. We'd go lion hunting instead.

After dropping Allen and Euni off at home, Mark and I hurried up the Mill Creek. We were on the track before noon, and Lee's dogs were released immediately. The track was so fresh that the dogs' baying soon became frantic. They had already jumped him.

As usual the cat led us over the roughest terrain he could find. We soon fell far behind, slipping and falling back at almost the same pace as we moved forward. Within a few minutes, however, the dogs barked treed at the top of a rugged cliff. To approach the tree we were going to have to inch around the cliff face for a few hundred feet before climbing up to the cornered cat. Mark and Lee made it to the top, but as they approached the lion, it leapt from the tree and bounded down through the hounds.

With blinding speed the cat was off the mountainside, across the narrow valley, and gone up the other side. The hounds bayed at his heels. He quickly treed again, this time a mile or more further up the drainage.

We slid and stumbled our way to the creek bottom, then began laboring up the other side. This time we didn't even get close before the cat jumped again—brave enough now to swat at the dogs as he passed through them. As we arrived on the scene, we found two of Lee's hounds bleeding and whimpering in pain.

Lee was now very upset. When a cat has the courage to come out of the tree onto the dogs, the dogs are in danger. He cussed, and said, "Shoot that SOB before he kills my dogs!" Of course that was what Mark had planned to do anyway. Now all he needed was the chance.

Unfortunately, this was not a large cat. In fact if he hadn't been such a danger to the dogs Lee would have probably collared them and gone home. But Lee was boiling mad, and we all knew that if Mark let the cat live it would be a danger on another day.

Within a mile or so the hounds were again barking treed. This time the cat had climbed the largest fir tree in sight, and was barely visible in its highest cluster of limbs. Mark's weapon was a single shot Remington Fireball pistol rechambered in a .222 caliber. He carefully took aim and squeezed off a shot. The troublemaker tumbled dead to the ground.

The day was now approaching dark. We trekked the several miles back down Mill Creek to the truck, tired but very satisfied. Mark insisted on dragging his trophy without help. As we walked, I put my arm across his shoulders.

Chapter 17

Alaska Caribou

Like so many hunters, the dream of an Alaska hunt had been with me for most of my life. In 1984 I traveled to Alaska for the first time. My son Mark and friends Ray and Ron went along. We did it up in a big way—hunting moose and caribou on the Wood River in the Alaska range and goats in the coastal mountains near the small town of Cordova.

Those hunts were filled with adventure and hardships, as we spent over a month in the bush without the aid of outfitters or guides. Mark later described our expedition in his book *The Joy of Misery*. But the trip was so successful we immediately began planning a second one—this time to include Allen and his friend Peter, Ray's son.

We wanted to see different country than we had before. We decided to hunt primarily for trophy caribou, and spend more time fishing. We also needed to get the boys back in time for school on September 2.

After months of considering our options, we decided to go to the Bristol Bay area of Southwestern Alaska. Our decision was influenced when I met Dave Egdorf at his home in Livingston,

Montana. Dave was a bush pilot that outfitted trophy fishing expeditions around Bristol Bay, and he knew the country as well as anyone. He told me that many trophy caribou lived in that area, and the fishing was unsurpassed. Soon we made a deal. He would fly us out to a small lake about 150 miles north of Dillingham, and then leave us to our own devices. We would float the Tikchik River for approximately sixty miles to the lower Nuyamaikak Lake for pickup ten days later. Two eight man rafts would be provided, and we would be responsible for everything else.

The river was only moderately fast and shouldn't cause us any real problems if we were vigilant. The only thing we would need to be very careful of were the grizzly bears.

The six of us left Livingston on August 14, 1986, in an old Dodge motor home. Our trip was to take us north through Banff and Jasper Parks, on through the increasingly magnificent Canadian Rockies to the Al-Can highway, across the Yukon Territory, and finally through Alaska to Anchorage.

Our flight from Anchorage to Dillingham was scheduled on August 18. I thought we made quite a spectacle as we carried duffles, tents, and boxes of groceries to the check-in counter. But no one seemed to notice—in Alaska I suppose this was commonplace. In fact, as we watched several native people check in, we saw everything from chickens in coops to goats on leashes. Later on the plane, several people held chickens and rabbits on their laps.

The flight went quickly and our gear arrived intact—except it carried an unusual goat-like odor. After the other passengers dispersed, we were left standing alone with our huge pile of gear. As we had come to expect from previous hunts, our pilot was nowhere to be seen. We didn't panic, just settled down to wait.

Hours passed until we were the only people left at the terminal. We were a long way from town, and there were no taxis. After the terminal closed for the day, we carried our stuff outside to wait. Mosquitoes and no-see-ums buzzed around our heads. Things weren't looking good, even by bush standards. After it started to rain, we decided to pitch our tents right by the terminal. But then up came a flashy pickup with Montana plates. Dave stepped out to say hello, but offered no explanation or excuses.

From Dawn Until Dusk

We made a fast trip into town for salt with which to prepare our capes then drove to a small lake nearby where two float planes waited.

We soon lifted off into the wilderness. Lakes, rivers, and vast forests passed under the wings. Crimson ribbons of spawning salmon decorated the rivers, and waterfowl of all sorts flushed as we passed over. We strained to spot a caribou, but saw nothing. Our hopes sank.

Before long Dave pointed ahead to a beautiful blue lake, shouting, "That's the one." As we began our descent, he gestured, then turned the plane toward a magnificent bull caribou standing alone in an open bog. Now we were ready to go!

Allen and I, in Dave's plane, circled and landed just behind the other plane. The pilots quickly taxied to a grassy shoreline. Within a few minutes our gigantic pile of gear was piled on the shore, high and dry. The pickup date was verified, and with goodbyes and some quick handshakes, they were gone.

We were alone in the middle of the Alaskan wilderness.

Since we were in excellent caribou country, we decided to pitch our first camp right there on the mossy lake shore. We quickly set up our tents and made our beds. Ron and Ray paddled out to fish for a few minutes. That night, however, we soon wished we had chosen our tent spots more carefully. Several football-sized rocks revealed themselves under the soft carpet of moss. We shifted around until we found man-sized shapes between the boulders.

Morning came with sparkling frost. It was a beautiful day with not a cloud in the sky. If we had known what the rest of our days were to bring, we would have appreciated it more.

Ron, Ray, and Peter decided to cross the lake to hunt for the bull we had seen from the air. Mark, Allen, and I headed off into the hills behind camp.

As always, the tundra that looked like a well-groomed lawn from above proved to be lumpy and boggy. The boys and I hunted for a couple hours and were circling back toward camp when Allen decided he would like to climb a nearby knoll to look over more country. My protective instincts balked, but I knew he needed to assert his own courage and skills. With a few words of caution I said okay.

While Allen climbed the rocky mountain, Mark and I trudged

on back to camp without having seen a single animal.

After a snack and a short nap, Mark and I paddled out into the lake to relax in the sun. I watched and worried for Allen. A few hours later we saw him coming along the lake shore toward camp. We paddled over to offer him a ride, and he filled us in on his afternoon experience.

No caribou, but he had seen a grizzly moving cross-country a long way off. We were excited to hear of the bear, but where were the caribou?

Soon the other guys came paddling across to camp with more news. After crossing a low ridge above the lake they had spotted two small caribou bulls. They had stalked the bulls, but had spooked them while still out of range. At least it was getting more interesting. Ron had also caught a five-pound Arctic char while crossing the lake. Just the right size for supper.

After a great fish dinner, we all decided to explore the fishing from the shore. Ron and I tried a great looking riffle just below the lake outlet while Ray wandered off downstream. Mark relaxed on the bank above us, looking the country over with binoculars. Allen and Peter napped in camp.

Suddenly Mark exclaimed, "There's a big bull!" Ron and I dropped our poles and ran up to him, but the bull had disappeared behind the hill above camp. Mark had his rifle with him, so he immediately headed off to intercept the caribou. We knew we couldn't keep up; Ron and I returned to fishing.

Ray had wandered around us on his way back to camp, and Mark intercepted him. They hustled on up the ridge toward the caribou. Soon we heard several shots, a pause, then another.

Ron and I dropped our poles and hurried toward them. From above, we could see them kneeling over a small bull caribou. Mark said, "He looked bigger from over there."

With congratulations to Ray, we got the rest of the story.

They had come to the top of the ridge but couldn't see anything. Just as they started to move, the bull had stepped out of the brush below them, turning to stare. In his excitement, Ray had emptied his rifle with no sign of a hit. Mark then passed Ray his rifle and advised him to lie down and take a rest before shooting again. By now the bull had moved off quite a distance. It paused once more

From Dawn Until Dusk

before crossing the next ridge. Ray fired and the caribou fell over dead.

After dressing and skinning it was back to camp with trophy number one and enough meat to last for several days.

Next morning we folded our tents and drifted off down the Tikchik River—our adventure now truly under way.

We needed to stay up in caribou country until we filled our tags, so we floated only a few miles before picking another campsite on a river bar. The river was shallow and wide up here, and the first day of floating was uneventful. This was good because we needed to get the feel for the boats before hitting the faster water below. We fished as we drifted, but the river seemed barren. Hordes of mosquitoes and no-see-ums swarmed around our heads, but the repellent kept them at bay most of the time.

The sky grew overcast, and drops of rain fell as we set up the tents. Rain would continue for the next seven days, almost without stop.

After soup and cheese sandwiches, we went hunting again. We split up as before, with Mark, Allen, and I going southwest and the others going southeast.

Visibility was limited, with fog and low clouds in all directions. Hardly were we out of sight of camp before shots rang out, echoing from the distant hills. I ran up on a nearby point and glassed toward the other hunters. A caribou bull stood on another little hilltop. I watched as he tipped over—just before another shot sounded. We decided to hunt on. They could take care of him.

We walked several miles to another lakeshore, circled the lake, and headed back toward the Tikchik. Every hilltop provided a panorama of the country ahead. Even though visibility was poor, we eventually spotted a caribou bull. He was at least two miles away and across the river, but he looked very big indeed. We quickly devised a plan to go after him. All we had to do was find a place to wade the icy river, bust through the extensive alder and willow thickets, and then cross two miles of tundra—all the while hoping the nomadic animal hadn't decided to leave Alaska.

Approaching where we had last seen him, our speed slowed. We looked the country over very closely. Just as we decided we

Allen's caribou bull was a team effort.

had lost him, a good set of antlers moved above the low brush across a small pond from us.

We had previously decided the first choice would be Allen's, and he definitely wanted this one. He and Mark bellied up for a rest while I stayed back to watch the action. The bull was unaware of us. Allen waited until the animal fed out of the brush and offered a clear shot. At the sound of the rifle the bull shuddered and turned around twice. He refused to fall, so Allen shot again. This time he crumpled and lay still.

We all did a little celebration dance with lots of shoulder slapping and congratulations. He had a beautiful double-shovel rack. His legs and body were dark chocolate brown, and his head and cape were pure white. The antlers were mature and hard, but still covered with chocolate-colored velvet.

As we finished photos and started field dressing, Ray came over the ridge and joined us. He had seen the same bull from across the river, and arrived on this side just in time to hear Allen shoot. We welcomed the help, and soon had the trophy and meat back to camp.

From Dawn Until Dusk

Peter ran out to meet us, anxious to tell us about the bull he had shot earlier. In three days we had bagged three caribou—not too bad! Three more to go.

The rain was getting to be a real nuisance. We were wet all day, and even our sleeping bags were getting damp. It was hard to find even a dry hour or two in which to salt our capes. One of the objectives of our trip was to get skins and antlers for our nascent wildlife museum in Livingston, and if the skins were to spoil much of our effort would be wasted.

Next morning found us on the river again. Our boats were beginning to sag under the load of meat, skins, and antlers. The rain had swollen the river, and so we moved faster with less effort. Fishing was still nonexistent, but the river looked fishier every mile.

Again we stopped early, but not as soon as we wanted. Camping spots were getting harder to find as the rising water covered the gravel bars. Now we were in a steep-walled canyon, with most potential camping spots covered by thick brush and larger trees. Finally we found an open gravel bar.

Since Mark, Ron, and I were still hunting, Allen and Peter stayed in camp playing cards while we ventured out. Ray accompanied Ron while Mark and I headed across the flat tundra to a distant range of hills.

We were almost into the hills when shots rang out through the foggy mist. Ron must have found some action. We hunted on.

We crept to the top of the first large hill. Instead of flat colorless tundra, a beautiful diorama opened before us. Lush meadows, lakes, and patches of trees spread around us. Standing knee deep in grass by a nearby lake were two magnificent bull caribou. The largest had a snow-white neck and mane, and the velvet on his huge antlers shone silvery gray through the rain. The second bull was also big, but nothing compared to the first.

The range was over eight-hundred yards. We dropped back over the ridge and circled downwind to approach from another direction. Again we were still much too far—and there was no cover that would allow for a closer approach.

We were stuck. After several minutes Mark wanted to try a shot, but I insisted we get closer. We started crab walking toward them, but we'd gone only fifty yards or so before the big bull came to full alert and turned toward us with his head up. The second bull followed his point, even though he hadn't seen us.

Mark ran forward to a rocky hump and dropped to his belly for a rest. Both bulls started moving away. Mark's first shot brought them around to attention.

"Aim right between the eyes," I said, thinking that at this distance he should compensate at least a couple of feet for the drop of the bullet.

A solid "whump" resounded on the second shot. Both bulls ran out of sight around the hill. I had a sick feeling that they were gone for good—after all these days and hard work.

We ran down toward them, and suddenly there stood a bull on the sidehill. Again Mark flopped down and fired. And again the bull ran around the hill out of sight.

We moved after him. And there in the bog lay the great, white-maned caribou—down but still alive. Mark moved closer. When he was about fifty yards from him, the bull rolled to his feet and threatened Mark with his head lowered and antlers swinging. A quick shot dropped him for good.

This was a really big bull. He dwarfed all the others. His antlers were thicker than my arms and almost as tall as Mark!

We skinned the cape and took the meat, and with darkness coming, headed back toward camp. Mark carried the huge antlers on his pack frame. It was almost dark before we finally spotted the orange ribbon we had tied on a pole above the tents.

Exhausted but happy, we stumbled into camp. Another large caribou head sat on the gravel bar. So that's what Ron had been shooting at. We quickly removed our soaked clothes and boots, and climbed into our damp-but-warm sleeping bags.

Next morning, after sleeping in and eating a leisurely breakfast in the rain, we tended to our hides, fleshing them out. As the rain let up that evening, we even had a chance to salt them down. Of course this allowed the bugs to again attack us in force.

Now we had a real load for our boats. Next morning they were piled high, and topped off with big antlers. With the hunt behind us, the adventure was yet to come, although of course we didn't know it at the time.

From Dawn Until Dusk

As we moved downstream, the river was getting stronger with each bend, and the gentle stretches were more often ending in white water.

Mark, Allen, Peter, and I were riding the big raft, with Mark doing almost all the rowing. Ron and Ray followed in the smaller raft with most of the meat and all the antlers. Mark had mastered control of our unruly craft, but Ray and Ron still hadn't learned to handle the smaller inflatable. They didn't seem to care where the water carried them. They relaxed, laughed, and drifted from bank to bank, totally out of control. Their oars usually lay unused inside the boat, while Mark worked constantly to navigate away from trouble.

Suddenly we rounded a bend and came upon a large fir tree down across the river. A narrow channel was open near the left bank, and Mark expertly guided our raft through it. We yelled out a warning to the other guys, but the current took them right into the center of the branches, dumping them and all the raft's contents into the frigid river.

We all knew the danger of being trapped underwater, held by the force of strong current. And so it was with great relief that we watched the raft, and then two heads, pop up below the sweeper. We rushed to salvage our trophies and gear, and soon had everything rescued and reloaded—with no loss or real damage.

As we continued down the river, Ron and Ray became a little more serious about the task they faced. We encountered other sweepers and several dangerous rapids, but had only one other potential catastrophe.

The river braided like a rope. Side channels split and split again before rejoining the main channel, sometimes within a few hundred yards but just as often miles downstream. If the rafts were to become separated we might never get back together again.

Just a couple miles after getting dunked, Ron and Ray drifted into a side channel. We looked back just as they floated out of sight down the other side, too late for either of us to do anything. We could only hope we drifted back together somewhere downstream. Hours later, when we had decided they were surely lost, they came drifting back into the main channel, singing aloud as if nothing had happened.

When the rain let up Peter and I began casting spoons into the deep pools. Pete soon had a big one on, and landed a five-pound Arctic char—bright and beautifully colored. Out came the rest of our poles. Soon all of us were catching fish, including Dolly Varden, salmon, and the largest grayling I had ever seen. For the rest of our trip downstream we caught fish whenever we wanted.

Most of our time in the boats, however, we sat humped under our rain coats, trying to stay warm. It was just too miserable to enjoy even such great fishing.

As we drifted on in dejected silence, Mark suddenly dropped the oars and grabbed at the gun lashed beside him. We all came to full alert. On an island just below us, a large black bear nosed at a dead salmon. We had bought black bear tags for just such a chance.

The bear disappeared into the brush. In hushed whispers I told Mark to slip out of the boat and ease down the far side of the island while we drifted down the other side, talking and making noise. At the lower end we beached on the gravel bar and waited. Soon Mark sauntered around the point, grinning widely. He told us that the bear had come out as planned, but just as he was getting ready to shoot he realized it was a grizzly—coal black but definitely a griz. Not legal for us but very exciting.

We were seeing more and more dead and partially-eaten salmon in the water and on the gravel bars. When we stopped for lunch we gathered wood among piles of dead salmon and huge mounds of bear dung. The tall grass on the banks was matted down with a network of bear trails.

After lunch we hadn't gone more than a mile when, as we came around a sharp bend in the river, we floated almost into the rump of a huge sow, fishing. She rushed out of the water, followed by half-grown twin cubs. As soon as she had pushed them into cover, she came back to the high bank above us and put on a hair-raising show! She roared, crashed branches, and threatened to jump into our boat. Our guns were lashed down and so we felt helpless, but we quickly drifted past, relieved to leave her behind.

Soon we spotted another, even larger bear in the river. He seemed almost indifferent to us, however, as he ambled up the bank and stood to watch us pass. A huge boar, with a head as big

From Dawn Until Dusk

as a washtub. He wasn't afraid of us . . . or of anything else.

The rest of that day and all of the next we saw bears of all shapes and sizes—boars, sows, and cubs. In two days we counted a total of twenty-five. And while they seemed a bit peeved with our intrusion, they all moved aside to let us pass.

As we saw more and more bears, we began to relax a little in their proximity. But none of us relished the idea of pitching camp in the middle of them. We found a small gravel bar with room for our tents between stinking salmon and huge piles of bear manure. After a quick meal we settled into our damp bags, guns and flashlights close by.

Sleep came quickly, but sometime during the night I jerked awake, blinking at total darkness. Just outside the tent, gravel crunched. Goose bumps erupted on my skin. I lay listening while our visitor moved off. Again all was quiet, and the next morning I inspected the gravel bar. A set of huge tracks circled our tents and bags of caribou meat. He hadn't touched a thing. He must have been so well fed on salmon and berries he had no interest in us or our meat. To show us his disdain, he had left a huge pile of berry-filled manure beside the tent.

We were soon on our way again, hoping to reach the lake that evening. The river grew deeper, wider, and much slower. About noon our progress was almost stalled as the wind blew hard upstream, right in our faces. To make any progress at all required heavy work at the oars. Mark insisted on doing all the rowing.

Just before dark we could see out from the river mouth to whitecaps on the lake beyond. We were here, and none too soon. Our rowers were exhausted.

Dave had instructed us to row out into the lake to an island for pickup, but the wind forced us to camp on mud flats at the river mouth. As we struggled to set up our tents, wind gusts inflated the nylon like parachutes. But we slept soundly that night, and the next morning saw that we again had been visited. Huge bear tracks circled our tents and gear, but nothing was disturbed.

This was the day scheduled for pickup, but the wind still roared off the lake. There was no way for us to get out onto the island. Dave would just have to pick us up here . . . we hoped!

About eleven in the morning a blue-and-white Beaver appeared on the southern horizon and circled the lake—then came our way. He passed over us and flew on up the river. Then around again. Now he dropped down and came in upwind, just over the water. But then he was up and circling again. Finally he touched down and taxied up to camp. An unfamiliar pilot stood out on a pontoon. "Okay guys, load up some stuff but save room for four guys. Dave will be here in a couple hours for the rest of the gear and the last two guys."

Ron and I opted to stay, suggesting that the others find rooms in town.

After they were gone, Ron and I packed two of the tents, deflated and folded the rafts, and readied everything else for departure. Dave would be here any time now, right?

We took a nap, shot at cans, and threw lures into the river. We played rummy, and waited, and waited. The afternoon was gone and dusk was coming fast. We heard planes, and saw planes off in the distance—but none came our way.

As darkness settled we resigned ourselves to another night with the bears and mosquitoes. But then with a roar and dip of wings, Dave landed straight in, taxiing right up to us. He hopped out and, with a big grin, grabbed a duffle bag.

As we loaded the gear, he explained the problems of landing on the river. Not only was there a danger of sticking in the shallows, but a floating log could wreck a plane.

Antlers were tied on the struts and the gear was stowed inside, Ron and I perched on top. With a roar we left the Tikchik, probably never to see it again. Suddenly the roar inside the plane became much louder. The right rear door had blown open. And my rifle was leaning there! Dave looked back, yelling, "Oh shit!" He dropped back to the lake surface, skipped around the plane to shut the door, and took off again. "No loss, all okay."

We flew for the next two hours in total darkness. After glimpsing the lights of Dillingham, we dropped down toward a slight glimmer on the pond ahead. I had no feeling or sense of distance, and was terrified that we would crash into invisible trees. But Dave gave us a perfect touchdown.

The guys were relieved to see us. After a hot bath and a dry bed we were off to Anchorage the next morning—and then the long, happy drive home.

Chapter 18

Dall Sheep in Northwest Territories

Rain splattered down from the clouds as we carried load after load of gear through the waist-deep water of Swamp Lake. With a final reminder of the pickup date, our grouchy pilot climbed into his old Otter twin and roared off, leaving us behind on this tiny patch of water.

August 15, 1988. Just another charter for Watson Lake Flying Service, but the beginning of a great Dall sheep adventure for our small group. There were four hunters, me and my friend Ron and my sons Mark and Allen. Our guides were Phil Merrill, a wildlife biologist from Alberta, and Rod Windorf, who farmed wheat, also in Alberta. Both proved to be capable outdoorsmen and great company.

Our plan was to set up base camp at Swamp lake, where we would store our emergency supplies and extra gear, and then hike out into spike camps for our hunting. As usual, things weren't quite what we had imagined from home. The mountains were much further away than we had thought, for instance, and we were separated from them by miles of dense timber, muskeg, and swamp.

We decided to split into teams. Mark, Ron, and Rod would go south into a small range between us and the Nahanni while Allen, Phil, and I would hike east through a low divide and up into Mitchell Creek. We would meet again in seven days at base camp to compare notes and regroup.

Swamp Lake had been chosen as our destination because, years earlier, another party of Montana hunters had taken trophy rams from Mitchell Creek, one of them a massive forty-two incher.

Next morning, after hugs and several "be carefuls," we parted company and trudged off with heavy backpacks into the fog and rain.

Six or seven miles later, Allen, Phil, and I emerged from the dripping forest onto one of the gravel bars of Mitchell Creek. The creek was swollen with rain, and would be an obstacle to cross. Since the day was late and we were tired, we decided to camp right there on the gravel bar.

Given the intermittent rain, we would find that the deep creek could vary by eighteen inches or more each day. It was sometimes easy to ford and sometimes quite difficult and dangerous. The creek water carried some glacial silt, but was still clear enough for us to see large grayling darting in the pools.

Our best avenue of travel would be the creek bed itself, even with its slick gravel and repeated crossings. The game trails along the creek made for relatively easy going.

The next day found us hunting up a major side drainage east, but the only game we sighted were four mountain goats clinging to a vertical rock face two thousand feet above us. That evening we decided to move camp another fifteen miles upstream. As we hiked, we noted fresh grizzly and wolf tracks on the sandbars. Except for a single cow moose and her calf, however, we saw little game. Our most pleasant diversion was picking through the abundant blueberry bushes along the creek.

The next day, less than an hour from camp, we spotted white sheep on the slopes far above us. Over fifty in all. As Phil and I had both hunted sheep before, we knew to expect no rams in this group. Nevertheless, we continued upward until we could see all of the huge, grassy basin. No rams. Only the ewes and lambs.

The disappointment was tough on Allen, and the physical stress was taking a toll on us all. We were wet and cold, and

From Dawn Until Dusk

decided on tea by a warm fire before heading back down to camp.

For the next three days we hiked and glassed until we had covered all of upper Mitchell Creek. We saw one large caribou bull alone on a sidehill across the valley, but decided to leave it. We were still at least thirty miles from Swamp Lake.

On the sixth day we spotted a white animal alone on a grassy sidehill. It looked goatish, but as we were going that way anyhow, we decided to go for him.

As we closed the distance, we saw that it was indeed a goat. A big one!

We approached around the mountainside, stalking to within two-hundred yards of the feeding billy. Allen bellied forward and found a rest in the boulders. A few minutes before, I had reminded him how important it is to anchor a goat, as they always seem to find a way to fall down some horrible precipice. Fortunately, this one appeared to be far from any cliffs.

The goat staggered with the first shot, and then fell with the second. He dropped out of sight. From our vantage, we hadn't been able to see that he was grazing at the head of a steep canyon. He had hung up on a brushy ledge just at the top of a hundred foot cliff. As we tried to extract him from the heavy brush for skinning, he slipped away from us and fell over and over onto the rocks below.

Miraculously, the face and horns were undamaged. Allen had a wonderful trophy goat; nine years old with nine-and-a-half inch horns. Only thirty-five miles from Swamp Lake.

Phil loaded his pack with the wet skin and head and staggered off down Mitchell Creek toward spike camp. Though Allen and I wanted to help, Phil would not give up the load. He eventually carried the heavy skin all the way back to Swamp Lake.

When we left the others, the plan had been to meet at Swamp Lake in seven days. It was late on the eighth day before we struggled back into base camp. The heavy packs had helped us cross a swollen Mitchell Creek, its waters nearly to our waists, but had slowed our return considerably.

As we dropped our packs, the sun shone through a spot in the clouds. Unzipping the tent fly, we discovered a note and a map. The message was, "We are okay. No trophy rams but lots of sheep with small rams. Have gone on to the range northwest of camp. Love you, Mark. PS. Pray you are okay, too."

Since they had hunted south and had now gone northwest, and since we had come from the east, the only place left for us to hunt was directly north of camp—across a wide valley of muskeg swamp and spruce timber.

This time we set up camp in a beautiful basin above timberline. We climbed a few hundred yards to glass as the sun dropped below the horizon. We saw a bear a mile or so below us, but no sheep.

Next morning we were up early and, with dawn, began glassing the basins and valleys. Even though this was classic sheep country—hanging grassy benches below sheer rock faces—we saw no sheep here, either.

My attention wandered, and I started looking at the mountains far off to the west—thinking of Mark and Ron and wondering if they were still okay.

My eyes were drawn to movement on a far off ridge. Two tiny stick figures crawled up toward a group of white dots. I called to Allen and Phil dozing nearby, "I see them!"

"See who?"

"Mark and Ron and sheep!"

Phil hastily set up the spotting scope and zeroed in. Sure enough, two men . . . and eleven rams.

While we watched, Mark and Ron lay flat on the slope. And then two sheep rolled over and lay still. The rest milled around in confusion until the men walked among them to their rams. The remaining sheep scattered up into the rocks.

Mark later told me that they had approached up to about 350 yards before the largest rams had stood and begun to move off. Ron had fired first and missed. Mark had then fired his 7 mm mag at the largest ram, which had collapsed on impact. Ron fired the second time and another ram fell. Mark's shot had broken the spine of his ram but Ron's ram was stone dead with no hole in his skin, only both eyes missing. The bullet had entered through one eye and exited through the other. Of course that's where Ron claimed he had been aiming.

Phil dug out his map and we determined they were seven miles from us. Since we hadn't found sheep and since there were nine more rams over there—and since we wanted to see those guys—

From Dawn Until Dusk

Mark posed with the exceptional rams he and Ron shot while Burl and Allen watched from across the valley.

we were off, practically running across the slopes. A couple hours later we came over a ridge above the creek valley. Their camp lay far below. Hurriedly, we dropped down to the creek and left our gear beside their tent. Carrying only rifles and binoculars, we hurried up the mountain toward them.

About halfway up, we heard voices in the brush, and soon met Ron, Mark, and their guide on their way down. It was a joyful meeting, with all of us excitedly trying to talk at once, telling stories from the last week. Finally we learned that among the nine other rams, at least one was a trophy.

They headed down the mountain while we went up to search for the other ram.

After finding the place where they had shot their sheep, we moved up to a high point and settled down to glass. Just before dark we saw a lone ram come down from the crags into a grassy basin and begin feeding. He was about two miles above camp.

Optimistic for the morning, we hurried down to our tents. Over sheep steak and mashed potatoes, we had a great evening by the fire.

Long before light, the three of us were out of camp and heading up the drainage. Phil was confident we would find the ram near where we had last seen him.

At first light we topped a ridge below the grassy basin, but no ram was in sight. We climbed and glassed, but still we could see nothing. Hope began to dwindle. But then Phil spotted him on a ridge far above us.

The ram was feeding around a rocky bench below a sheer cliff—barely visible against a background of gray rocks. Ducking back out of sight, we circled behind the ridge for a couple hundred yards and then peeked over again. We were as close as we were going to get, but he was still a long way away.

Allen lay in the rocks and, to settle his pounding heart, clicked on an empty chamber. Once, twice. Then he chambered a round and took a deep breath.

Boom! A miss! The ram turned in confusion. "Low," I whispered.

Boom! A hit! As the whack of the bullet echoed back to us, the ram staggered out of sight. Allen and Phil hurried over the ridge while I gathered cameras and packs.

Soon another shot echoed. I followed them to find a beautiful white ram lying at Allen's feet. Phil seemed almost as elated as Allen—I suppose he was glad to finally conclude our ten day marathon with a beautiful, full-curl ram.

Our last discussions with the guys at camp had been that they

From Dawn Until Dusk

Allen and Burl with a hard-earned ram.

should leave without us if we hadn't returned by noon. But since we now had our ram early, the rush was on to get the skinning and meat preparation finished quickly. After our joyful reunion yesterday, I hated to think of the long hike back without them.

As we approached camp, the men were just preparing to pack out. They were thrilled to see Allen's ram horns riding the top of his pack.

After congratulations and a brief rest, the six of us shouldered our packs and started home. The five hour hike passed very quickly, and the big blue tent in base camp looked like the Hilton after all those nights in three man tents.

Next morning dawned bright and sunny. A good day for flying—or just being alive in this beautiful valley. We prepared

Back row, from left to right, guide Phil Merrill, Burl Jones, and guide Rod Windorf. Front row, left to right, Mark Jones, Ron Thompson, and Allen Jones.

---

camp for departure, but did not pack the tent—just in case. By noon the plane still had not arrived. Phil said that if it hadn't come by noon it wouldn't come that day at all. We unpacked our little two-man raft and went fishing.

By the evening of the third day in camp, conversation drifted to stories of lost planes and forgotten hunters. Winter was coming, and it was a long hike indeed to the road—about 150 miles south to Tungsten. We had plenty of food and clothing but the Nahanni River was between us and safety. A formidable obstacle.

The next morning dawned again with clear skies. Why couldn't we have had some of this weather when we were hunting? In boredom and growing concern, we all watched the sky and listened for an engine.

The morning of the fourteenth day was clear but colder, and a change in the weather could be felt. By ten o'clock a huge cloud bank loomed to the northwest and wind sighed in the spruce

From Dawn Until Dusk

trees.

Ron had begun to joke again, hoping to lighten things up a bit. He challenged anyone to bet that the plane would not be here again before noon. Allen took the bet. And at 11:55 we all were alerted by a distant drone. It soon materialized into a plane passing over. At first we feared he was just passing through, but then he circled beyond the lake and glided onto the water.

We all checked our watches. The plane touched down thirty seconds before noon!

This was not our Otter but a small Beaver. Six people would not be able to fly in this plane.

The pilot climbed out onto the pontoon. "Hunters, pile in here quickly. A storm is coming!"

As we waded to the plane, he explained to Rod and Phil what was happening. The Otter had blown an engine at Watson Lake, and the storm had already dumped a foot of snow at Little Dall Lake. If we didn't hurry we would be stranded here . . . maybe for a long time. He would fly the hunters to Tungsten on the border and return immediately for the guides and gear.

By the time we landed on Flat Lake at Tungsten, snow blew sideways, reducing visibility to a few feet. The plane roared off to the north again.

Fortunately, the storm hadn't yet developed at Swamp Lake. The pilot made it out with our friends, and flew them to Watson Lake ahead of the storm.

Because of the bad weather, a truck was sent for us. But to reach the truck, we had to cross frigid Flat Lake, all of us packed into a fourteen-foot fishing skiff. Water lapped inches away from the gunwale. We made it to shore safe enough, but from there had to ride another two hundred miles over rough and rutted mud roads to civilization. Six hours later, we were checking into our motel.

As Mark said later, "A fitting end to a tough hunt."

Chapter 19

Sheep, Moose, and Bear in British Columbia

For folks living in moose country, these huge deer often provide a full year's supply of quality protein. Not only are they a source of meat, they are often a nuisance as well. On two occasions moose provided me with more excitement than I wanted.

In the spring of 1988 I was on a grizzly bear hunt with Big Nine Outfitters in northern British Columbia. My hunting partner was Bob Coffee, a new friend from California who had recently bought a vacation home in Montana. Bob and I had driven to Fort Nelson from Montana, and were met there by our host, Barry Tompkins. From Fort Nelson we flew into our hunting lodge.

Our hunt was to be on horses from the main lodge. We would each have our own guide, and hunt independently in different directions. We were the only hunters in camp, and our guides the only personnel. Barry had business elsewhere and left as soon as we had unloaded our gear.

My guide, whom I'll call "Lee," had spent the winter in camp, running a trap line for wolves and lynx. Bob's guide, "Ted," was a younger fellow and had come into camp just a day or two before us—but he seemed to be capable and experienced. We were both

From Dawn Until Dusk

optimistic and ready to go shoot big bears.

As we unloaded our gear, I noticed that Barry had brought a large box for Lee, a care package from his mother. Lee seemed very happy to see the gift, which unfortunately contained (as we would soon find out) a fifth of Kentucky's best.

By first light the next morning we had finished breakfast and had the horses saddled. Lee and I rode up the river west of the lodge. Our objective was a distant mountain with an open, south-facing slope. We hoped to spot a grizzly feeding in the newly-greened grass.

After about a two-hour ride, we dismounted in a beautiful little basin at the foot of a wide open slope. We settled in with our binoculars, planning to watch the mountainside until late in the day or until a bear showed itself. But we had been there only a few minutes when Lee said, "I just remembered I was supposed to bring in a couple of spare horses for tomorrow. I have to go back to camp. You stay here and keep on glassing. I'll be back by mid-afternoon."

This seemed a little strange and irresponsible to me. We had just met, after all, and he had no idea if I was capable of being there alone, especially if a griz showed up. But I didn't argue, and he quickly mounted up and was gone. I settled in for a long day, quite happy to be there alone. The day was warm and sunny, and the country was beautiful. Cow elk soon started to feed out from the brush far up the mountainside. There were no calves in view, but this time of year I knew they had to be close. The cows stayed near the low brush where the calves were probably hidden.

After a while the cows all jerked to attention, staring around the mountainside to my left. I swung my binoculars to follow their eyes . . . and saw a bear loping straight toward the cows. My excitement soon cooled, however, as the bear was obviously a black bear, and not a large one. I settled down to watch the drama unfold.

Clearly the bear was after the calves. The cows moved to block his path. He circled and tried to approach from another direction, but the cows blocked him again. After several minutes and much maneuvering, the cows tired of their little game, and attacked the bear. Wisely he retreated, running for his life. The elk returned to peaceful grazing.

The day passed without further excitement, and as the sun set a chill settled into my little hideaway. Since Lee hadn't returned I decided to build a fire and gather enough wood to keep it going all night if needed. I knew how to ride back to the lodge but I was afraid I might miss him in transit.

As darkness approached I decided something was wrong. But now it was too late for me to ride back in this wild country. Just as I settled in for the night I heard a horse coming into my clearing. It was Ted. He quickly helped me saddle my horse, then explained our problem as we rode back home.

It seems that Lee simply couldn't resist the pull of that giant bottle of whiskey, and had drunk himself unconscious, barely able to tell Ted where he had left me. Ted apologized over and over, but I assured him no harm had been done, not knowing then that Lee would stay drunk for the rest of my trip.

Our guides did not know when Barry would be back, and they had no way of getting in touch with him. The next day I waited in camp while Bob and Ted continued their hunt. By mid-morning on day three, boredom forced me to saddle up my horse and head out on my own—not a wise decision, but better than wasting my time in camp.

Again I rode up the river with a plan to look over the same mountainside as the first day. But I was just a couple miles from camp and riding through a lodge pole thicket on a very narrow trail, when the brush crashed ahead of me. A huge cow moose came charging out, her hair bristling and her ears flattened. My horse whirled and sprinted back down the trail with the moose on his tail and me hanging on for dear life. As we galloped into the open, my horse picked up speed and soon left our pursuer behind. With difficulty I convinced my trembling mount to stop, and turned to watch the moose go back into the thicket. Most horses are terrified of moose, and this one was no exception.

I sat on the horse and watched my back trail. The cow soon emerged on the hillside above the thicket with a small calf at her heels. They crossed the open hillside and went over a low ridge, down toward the river canyon below. With much urging I convinced my horse again to enter the thicket, and eventually to follow the moose toward the river.

The ridge provided a grand view of the river valley and the

From Dawn Until Dusk

mountainside across. I tied my horse off and settled down to enjoy the scenic panorama.

While I watched, the cow and her baby emerged from the brush below and stood on the riverbank. She was obviously intent on crossing the swollen current, but the calf was equally determined to stay on shore. Finally he lay down. She waded across, leaving him alone on the riverbank. I watched as she climbed the far mountainside and crossed the ridge out of sight.

I couldn't believe she had actually abandoned her baby; and indeed within a few minutes she came back down the mountain and across the river. She nudged the calf onto his feet, but he still refused to enter the water. She left him again. This time she stood on an island in the middle and called back to him over and over. The calf answered, but refused to budge.

Back she came again, and this time she actually nudged him into the water. While she waded, he swam and drifted downstream. Eventually they both arrived on the island again, and he flopped down, exhausted and trembling, soaked with the frigid water.

Again she left him, and again she crossed the mountain. This time I thought she was gone for good, but after thirty minutes she came back and crossed over to the island. She forced the little guy to his feet and into the water. He bravely tried to follow her across, but this time the strong current swept him under. She stopped on the far bank, waiting in vain for him to reappear. She soon left, crossing the mountain. She did not come back.

My time in those beautiful mountains in May of 1988 was interesting in many ways, but neither Bob nor I saw a grizzly bear. Lee stayed drunk until his whiskey ran out, and when Barry flew in a few days later he was furious, and very apologetic to me—but it was too late for a successful hunt. Since I had a sheep hunt scheduled for the coming fall, Barry volunteered to add a grizzly to my program free of charge. I was satisfied with that.

The following September found me again in the Big Nine area, this time with Ron Thompson, my old hunting buddy. Ron was along to be the "photographer."

My primary objective was now the beautiful, gray-black stone sheep, and my guide for these ten days was the very energetic and colorful Ben McBee. Ron and I had a great time with Ben, and his tall tales and exuberance kept us entertained the whole time.

Shortly after meeting Ben at the lodge, we watched him corral a green, three-year-old gelding. After a few hours of intensive work, he saddled the frisky colt and rode him around the corral, then into the field. Next day this colt was his mount as he led us and our pack string from the lodge and over the mountains to our first destination—Sloan Gulch, famous for its big stone rams.

Our journey took all day, and we pitched our spike camp along the creek just as the sun dropped behind the mountains. Ben hobbled the horses and pushed them on up the valley, the idea being that our camp would block them if they tried to return home. He also placed a cowbell on the dun colt he had ridden. The horse hadn't quite figured out his role yet, and had caused a little trouble all day. But considering this was the first day he had ever been ridden, he did remarkably well. We were very impressed with Ben's ability as horse trainer, wrangler, and guide. Now we were anxious to see if he could cook as well. We were starved, since we'd had only granola bars since our predawn breakfast in the lodge.

He soon had us fed, and while he checked the horses, Ron and I washed dishes and prepared lunch for tomorrow—we didn't want to miss lunch again!

We settled down into our sleeping bags, exhausted. After what seemed like only a minute, we were awakened by galloping horses, a clanging bell, and a running, cussing cowboy in white long johns and cowboy hat. The horses had come right through camp and were headed home, hobbles, bells, and all. Ben was dead after them, running and cussing through the rocks and timber in total darkness.

There was nothing we could do, so Ron and I snuggled back down into our bags and went back to sleep. After an hour or two we were again awakened as Ben came limping barefoot back through camp, leading two horses and pushing the others ahead. This time he tied his colt and one other, and pushed the others up the valley again.

By now it was almost time to get up, but Ben was exhausted. Ron and I kept quiet so he could sleep until the sun drove him out.

From Dawn Until Dusk

It was almost noon when we finally rode from spike camp and up into a beautiful, high mountain valley. As promised we immediately started seeing rams. There were rams on both sides, but they were all quite high, almost on the top. We could see a dozen or more at one time, and several looked to be full curl and legal. Barry wanted to take rams as old as possible because Fish and Game awarded additional tags if an outfitter's tagged rams were ten years or older.

We rode further up the valley, stopping every few minutes to glass—hoping to find a big ram lower on the slopes. But all of the rams we could see were so high that they paid little attention to us, and there was no way to approach them over the open terrain. Finally we spotted a big ram near the head of the basin.

He was feeding in some low brush. A boulder field offered some cover for our approach. Through the spotting scope he looked to be nearly forty inches on the curl, and was at least ten years old.

We tied the horses in a small grove of aspens a half mile from the ram and began our stalk. About three hundred yards from our target we ran out of cover. With a solid rest, I felt that I could make the shot. The boom from my old Sako .300 Win mag echoed from the surrounding slopes. My stone sheep toppled over. Our first day out and I had a beautiful, dark ram. Now we could concentrate on that grizzly bear, and possibly a moose.

Next day we broke camp and rode with my trophy back to the lodge, ready and anxious to find a bear.

Our next destination was a long valley across the river to the south, where the tracks of a very large bear had been appearing regularly. Again we took a spike camp with plans to stay out for the duration of my hunt.

As we moved into our hunt area, we began to see fresh bear sign on the trails ahead of us. We expected to jump him at any moment.

We chose a good campsite, and, after getting things in order, hiked up onto the side hill to glass the valley above us. We saw no bears, but a bull moose made a racket in the aspen thicket a mile or so above camp. Two cow moose wandered out to feed just below us as the sun dropped from sight.

Next morning, with great optimism, we quietly saddled and

Ron Thompson, left, and Burl, with Burl's fine stone ram.

rode slowly up the valley, fully alert. Ben rode ahead, then me, with Ron behind.

Ben gradually widened the distance between us, even though he stopped to glass frequently. Before we had gone a mile, he was a hundred feet or more ahead, and was out of sight in the timber. Suddenly he came galloping back down the narrow trail, cussing and shouting. "Shoot that sonofabitch! Shoot him!"

Ben streaked past us. My horse twisted and bucked, and I soon fell flat into the mud. But I had managed to hold onto my rifle. As I rolled over onto my feet, I looked up into the face of—not the bear I expected, but a very angry and belligerent bull moose. He was a youngster with a small rack, not an animal I wanted to shoot. He hesitated a moment, and after just a few seconds decided he really didn't like us being there. With a bellow and deep grunt, he lowered his head and charged.

He had given me just enough time to chamber a cartridge and

From Dawn Until Dusk

settle down. I calmly shot him ... through the right antler. He fell back, shook his head vigorously, and stepped off the trail to circle around us, grunting ominously. But he had already decided not to mess with these strange critters any more.

I looked around for Ron and Ben, but neither was in sight. I yelled for Ron, and he answered from far up the hillside. I soon saw him coming down through the thick aspens. His horse had bolted and run panicked through the trees with Ron hanging on and ducking tree limbs. Ben came riding calmly back up the trail with a sly grin. "Did you shoot that nasty little bastard?"

We continued up the valley, but now with little hope because of the uproar the moose generated. As expected we saw no bears in that valley, even though we hunted there the rest of the week. And after that first day we saw no more fresh tracks. The smart old bear had moved out.

Each morning we came up that same trail on our way to hunt, and each morning that little bull moose challenged us, but always backed off, grunting.

We had learned that a rutting bull moose can cause big trouble, and he had learned something as well.

Chapter 20

Someday

Ptarmigan flushed across the wide, windswept valley. At least a hundred of the pure white grouse (mottled brown with a changing season) rose with a fluttering roar—some so close that my horse jumped sideways, nearly dislodging me from my seat.

We were working our way above timberline to the hunting country of the Yukon's Ogilvie Mountains. My son, Mark, and I were being guided by Marty Thomas through vistas of snow-covered slopes, craggy peaks, valleys of dwarf alder, beaver dams, and rolling muskeg. Hundreds of miles of this could be glassed from a high ridge with not a living thing in sight. The low brush was higher than it appeared, and could hide bull caribou and moose completely.

We were to do our hunting and packing entirely from horseback, at least until game was spotted. Up before dawn to gather the horses, a quick breakfast, a packed lunch, and then a ride out from the spike camp in a new direction . . . this would be our schedule for the next ten days.

Our string included five pack horses and three saddle horses. Marty was an expert packer as well as an excellent guide, and

From Dawn Until Dusk

we experienced no serious difficulties in those ten days. My horse was some trouble for me because he was tall and skittish, but he was a genius at negotiating the muskeg and bogs.

Our first day consisted mostly of a five-hour trip down the upper Hood River and up Moose Creek to the luxurious Moose Valley Lodge—a plywood shack about eight feet by sixteen feet, with a Visqueen window, tin stove, and a bear-crunched plywood door.

The hunt began in earnest with the next day's ride up Moose Valley. Given our sore butts and knees and the lack of game, the ride seemed longer than it was. A couple of miles above camp, in the fresh snow, we saw the tracks of a bull caribou headed down the valley. "We must have ridden right by him," Marty remarked with surprise.

As we returned later in the day and were approaching camp, Mark spotted movement against the hillside far ahead. He whispered to me, "Caribou." We dismounted and pulled out our binoculars. The bull fed contentedly in a large mineral lick, unaware of us. Marty set up his spotting scope. After only a few seconds, he whispered, "This is a keeper. You'd better take him if you can."

Mark and I agreed and started our stalk through the taller brush along the creek bank. We spotted him at four hundred yards, then again at two hundred yards. Mark crept closer. One hundred yards separated him and his quarry. Mark eased out of the brush. The bull spotted him just as he steadied his rifle on a limb. The shot echoed, and the bull pitched forward and lay still. The 139 grain hand load from Mark's 7 mm mag had done an excellent job, as it had so many times previously. The bull was humanely dead before he had been aware he was in trouble.

The antlers proved to be exceptionally long and heavy with good point development—and miraculously did not shrink as we approached. In fact they seemed to grow. Before our hunt ended we were to see and evaluate a dozen or more mature bulls, but none as good as this first one.

The third morning dawned clear and cold and found us packing camp to move out of Moose Valley into Grizzly Valley, five hours down Hart River. Since we had bagged a caribou from Moose Valley, we hoped to bag a moose from Grizzly Valley; it sounded reasonable at the time.

Griz camp was a duplicate of the Moose Lodge—a plywood box on the banks of a clear mountain creek. The scattering of stunted trees provided shelter and firewood; the grassy meadows made good feed for the horses; and the ptarmigan provided a potential change of menu.

As the sun was already below the horizon, we were content to simply hobble the horses and settle into camp. A good warm fire, hot chocolate, caribou steaks, fried potatoes, and sweet corn hit the spot. After dinner, we listened to Patsy Cline on Marty's portable tape player and told our respective bear stories.

My own story had roots twenty-eight years old, when Mark was five months old and my wife, Eunice, and I moved to Saint Ignatius, Montana. As a twenty-four-year-old dental school graduate, I was sent by the Division of Indian Health to the Flathead Indian Reservation.

For me, heaven was in those shining mountains. I learned taxidermy and spent my thoughts and time hunting and fishing—while Euni graciously tolerated it all. I spent hundreds of hours alone or with Indian companions in the canyons and peaks.

After nearly two years of this kind of constant exposure, my two-year-old son had learned to identify by name all the big game animals in the Rockies. But Eunice and I were still surprised by Mark's first complete sentence.

We were driving along the face of the Missions, Mark standing between us on the seat, when he said, pointing a tiny finger toward the peaks, "Someday me kill a bear in those high big mountains."

After twenty-six years of frustration, disappointment, and a pair of my own botched attempts, an opportunity for Someday had come for Mark and me. But who could have guessed that it would come in Yukon's Ogilvie Mountains—so far from our home in Montana.

The fourth morning, we headed up the valley with great

From Dawn Until Dusk

anticipation. A crisp, frosty morning with a two-day-old snow and the promise of sunshine seemed a great beginning.

On a previous hunt, large bear tracks had been seen three miles above the grizzly camp in the area of two recently-taken moose carcasses. Marty was optimistic, and had Mark and I ready for action.

Marty didn't know the exact location of the carcasses, so we grew cautious as we approached the general area. With rifles ready we slipped quietly along, pausing to look and listen before each step. Finally from a little knoll next to a dense thicket, Marty howled like a wolf, hoping to bring a bear out into the open to protect his cache.

Silence. Nothing. We zeroed in on the ravens and slipped in to find the carcasses untouched by anything but birds. A large wolverine had approached and circled the remains, but had moved on without feeding.

Disappointed, we continued up Griz Creek for a full day of moose hunting.

That day ended with only a few moose tracks and an ebbing of confidence. The next day began with a herd of fifty caribou across from camp. The bulls chased cows and fought each other. We noted with satisfaction that there was nothing there as large as the bull that Mark had taken. This day ended poorly as well. We followed a fresh bull moose track through bogs and brush for five hours, only to have it finally outdistance us.

We had reached the halfway point on our hunt and had yet to see a moose or even a sign of a bear.

Pete Jensen, our outfitter, had already taken six bears that fall—more than usual. And according to Marty, they had never taken a bear as late in the year as we were hunting. As bears near hibernation, they travel less and stay closer to the den, making them much more difficult to find.

Day six found us in the gray of predawn far down in the Hart River valley, riding around beaver ponds and through large stands of fir and poplar. A blue sky stretched from horizon to horizon. It was a great day to be alive and in the Yukon.

But there were no bears. The closest we came was a blondish cow moose and her blonder calf, traveling alone. And then a white spot, shining in the browns of the muskeg, that became a good bull caribou approaching us from across the valley.

The morning of the seventh day began as the previous six had, with Marty frying bacon and brewing cowboy coffee before Mark and I had even put our feet on the frozen floor. After breakfast, Mark and I helped clean up and prepare for another day.

The day's plan had been conceived with less enthusiasm than before. We intended to hunt across a high pass above camp—the last area from camp that we hadn't covered—with the hopes of seeing a moose. We all seemed to be losing interest. After three months away from his wife and family, Marty was ready to put out the fire and call in the dogs.

As Mark made lunch, I leaned against the door frame and glassed the hills across from camp; an old die-hard that hates to give up.

Marty joined me and began to glass the same hillsides. I dropped my binocs back to my chest in resignation. Marty glassed well above snowline, higher than where I had been searching. He knew about a caribou carcass from a previous hunt, a spot that should have been insignificant given the moose carcasses in the valley. But after only a moment, he said, "We got us a bear."

Mark popped out the door, bread bag in hand. "What did you say?"

I stared at then both before raising my glasses to the mountain again. From nowhere and beyond hope . . . a griz! A griz in the snow on the hump of the caribou carcass.

Mark and I wanted to head out immediately. Mark even suggested starting off on foot from camp, even though the horses were saddled and the bear was two miles away and two thousand feet up.

But Marty settled us down, insisting that the bear was not going anywhere for a while.

With a lunch packed in our saddlebags, we were soon off, hurrying across the valley, laboring up the steep slopes, winding through the bogs and dwarf spruce to a point several hundred yards below and around from our quarry.

We tethered the horses, chambered cartridges, and began our stalk through deep snow and loose rocks. As quietly as possible, we raised ourselves over the rocky ridge and peered into the snowy basin. No bear.

From Dawn Until Dusk

It had to be a miscalculation. Maybe it was the wrong basin. He had to be just over the next ridge. Had to be.

By the time we reached the next highest point, we were sweating through our wool and eating quick handfuls of snow.

Again we crept to the edge and peered over into the basin. And again, no bear. We moved forward a few steps to see into the upper part of the basin. I saw in Mark's face the same kind of dejection that I was sure was in my own.

But then . . . Marty tensed and pointed, easing down into a crouch. "There."

The bear was stretched out asleep across a hump of dirty snow—what was left of the carcass after he had fed and covered it back up. Even at a distance, we could make out the luxurious length of its fur and the size of its head, cocked at an angle down the hill.

For the outfitter, it is very important to shoot a boar and not a sow. According to governmental regulations, a sow is worth three points and a boar one—so an outfitter can take three times as many bears if they are all male.

Although it is impossible to be sure, a bear alone will usually be male. We had to take our chances.

Mark bellied up and rested the .338 across his camera pack. The bear lay flat, partly behind the mound of snow with his vital areas shielded. Not an easy shot.

"Should I howl and get him up?" Marty whispered.

Mark shook his head. "I don't want him moving."

After sucking another gulp of air, Mark squeezed the trigger. I sat slightly away, prepared to back him up if necessary.

The .338 bucked and the boom echoed across the basin. The bear jumped up and looked around, surprised. He started loping around the mountainside above us, obviously confused and not knowing which way to go.

Mark fired a second shot. His bullet smacked solidly. The big animal tumbled forward into the deep snow only to bounce immediately up and come plunging down the mountain toward us.

Mark squeezed off another shot at the rapidly-closing animal. At the report, the bear tipped forward and dug a trench in the snow with his nose, skidding several feet before coming to rest on

Hunting guide Marty Thomas, left, and Burl, with Mark's fall Yukon grizzly.

---

his belly with all four legs spread. He didn't move again.

The .338 had broken the near shoulder and ranged back through the lungs and liver to lodge under the skin on his left hip. The first hit was a little far back and just below the spine: fatal, but not a stopper.

Mark and I stood and stared at each other in disbelief. We reached out and grasped hands. He had done it!

We approached cautiously, but the bear was obviously quite dead. A beautiful grizzly, as pure a symbol of the wilderness as you will find. All those trips over the years, all those miles of floating and horsebacking, and then the final moment of triumph. A hundred moments of anticipation and disappointment had certainly been worth this one moment of achievement.

The fur had a kind of honey-color to it, with darker legs and hump, and was five-inches deep. We lifted a leg and felt through the fur. A boar.

Mark and I tackled the skinning while Marty returned to

From Dawn Until Dusk

bring up the horses as close as possible. By the time he returned, we had the skinning down to the removal of the paws and head. Marty thought it a real treat to have taxidermists as clients. We, in turn, felt fortunate to have an experienced guide that was also an all-around good guy.

Spread on the snow, the skin squared seven feet. And a biologist later aged the skull at seven to eight years.

Marty packed the skin onto his horse and we headed on out, back to camp.

The next day as we pulled out for the last time, I couldn't resist one final look at the snow-covered mountainside, the site of yesterday's excitement. Nothing but ravens fed there. We turned the horses down Griz Creek and toward home. They needed no urging, seeming to know that this was the last day.

About two hours down the trail we came face to face with a bull moose. At forty yards, we stood and sized each other up.

Mark turned in his saddle, and softly asked, "Should I?"

Though his antlers spread over fifty inches, I shook my head. "Naw."

We had the trophy of our Someday, and didn't really need another. We would leave that moose on the high big mountain for somebody else's dream.

Part III

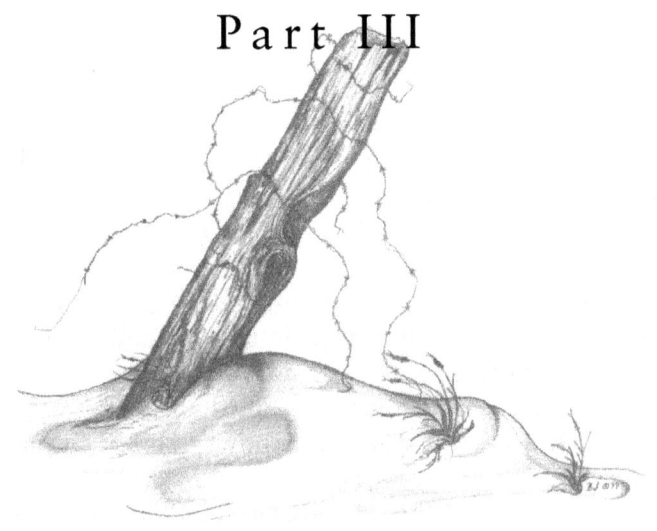

Chapter 21

Foreign Lands

For a hunter of a certain ambition and mind-set, adventures at home naturally lead to travels in foreign lands. For the Jones family, our first overseas destination was Namibia.

We met our host at a hunt show in Charleston, West Virginia. Gillie Bredencamp had placed a handwritten sign in his booth: "Cheapest hunt in Africa." This caught my attention, and soon we had a deal. For a relatively modest sum, the boys and I could each take ten animals. We would stay in his ranch house and he and his son would be our guides. The year was 1989. Most of the hunting was relatively tame compared to what we would experience later, but it was a fantastic introduction to Africa. The boys and I each took kudu, gemsbok, warthog, zebra, hartebeest, blesbok, springbok, jackal, and steinbok.

Several years later, and with the African bug firmly implanted in us all, we booked a second trip, this time to South Africa's Northern Transvaal with Ken DuPlessis. Again we all went, this time with Mark's partner, Michaela, as well. Only Mark and Allen hunted on this trip. They each took waterbuck, bushbuck, and impala, and Mark bagged a mountain reedbuck, a baboon, and a vervet monkey.

In 2001 Mark, Allen, and I traveled to Zimbabwe to hunt on Lake Kariba. Mark hunted almost everything the area had to offer, bagging lion, leopard, elephant, hippo, crocodile, warthog, bushbuck, Cape buffalo, and sable. Allen shot a Cape buffalo and sable, and had a very close encounter with a charging buff.

Most recently Mark and I traveled to the swamps of Mozambique to hunt Cape buffalo, nyala, bushbuck, red duiker, bush pig, and various other small antelope. This time our companion was our friend Dr. J. D. Bailey from West Virginia.

Between Zimbabwe and Mozambique, Mark and I traveled to the Kamchatka Peninsula of Eastern Russia for brown bears. We flew in on huge, vintage military helicopters and spent most of the time hiking on top of six feet of snow. We both bagged nine-foot plus boars with beautiful thick coats.

Mark, Allen, and I hunted Fannin's sheep in the Yukon, and Coues deer in Chihuahua, Mexico. Allen and I hunted whitetails near Mountain House, Alberta, and Mark and I hunted whitetails in Northern Manitoba and big moose and goats on the Turnagain River in British Columbia. I also accompanied Mark for moose and caribou in the Yukon.

All of our travels have had several purposes. Not only have we shared good times and adventures, but I've always taken extensive photographs, measured the dimensions of our animals, and studied their habits and movements—all for the sake of recreating them in sculpture and taxidermy.

Most of my sculpture has been a direct result of exposure to living subjects. Hunting, dissecting, and studying animals in their wild habitat has proven critical to my rendering of these animals in bronze. With every new hunt, every new experience, I've found that some aspect of my work has angled off into a new and exciting direction.

To this date I have completed over two hundred significant sculptures. The work has become a large part of who I am. To not have a project underway leaves me feeling confused and directionless. The art has fed my life in much the same way that my life has fed the art. I can't imagine a better or more fulfilling way to spend my days.

Chapter 22

Mozambique

by Dr. Mark S. Jones

In July of 2005, Dad and I, along with our friend J. D., went to Mozambique to hunt Cape buffalo and several other species.

Thirteen years after the end of a brutal bush war, Mozambique was finally starting to crawl back to a place where it could host a mixed-bag hunt. During our ten days in the 280-square-mile concession, we hunted suni and red duiker in thick jungle, hartebeest and eland in flood-plain palm trees, and Cape buffalo in swamp. Lions came and went, while elephants took refuge in the forest. Leopards lunched on the many forest duikers and pigs. As we hunted, we saw evidence of all the big four. Poachers, the most vicious predators of all, were also in evidence.

From Johannesburg we flew into Beira, Mozambique, and then flew forty-five minutes in a Cessna 205 to our comfortable camp on the Mangari River. A young professional hunter named Glen Haldane would be guiding Dad and me while an Afrikaaner named Awie (Arvie) would be J. D.'s PH.

While we all arrived as intended, my rifle unfortunately trailed along somewhere behind us. I started hunting with Awie's old Sako .308, complete with a Tasco scope and some very dubious-looking military ammo. The solid bullets had differing weights and were in various stages of decay, from polished brass to green to black. The cases still bore link belt marks. I hoped we would only be hunting duiker until my guns arrived.

J. D.'s rifle had arrived in good order, and after a couple of shots to ensure that his new .416 was still accurate, he was ready for anything. In addition to the buffalo and little stuff, he was going to try for a Roosevelt's sable. It was shaping up to be a great hunt, despite my not yet having my big gun.

Our first full day of hunting was spent cruising the roads and grassy pans looking for suni, red duiker, and bush pig. It didn't take long before a suni crossed the road ahead of us. It stood quietly behind a screen of leaves. I shot at what I could see of him, which wasn't much. My shot wasn't perfect, and I had to chase down the little ten-pound antelope and finish him off with a knife. He was a record book head, with horns that extended past his ears.

Later on in the hunt, we would walk the forest roads slowly, staring into the brush for a flash of red or a twitching tail that would give away a suni. I killed two more book rams in this manner, but the shooting was always difficult.

Flushing bush pigs was a more exciting proposal. Our hunting concession contained many dry ponds surrounded by rings of tall, coarse grass. The grass was six to ten feet tall and often extended for hundreds of yards around a central depression. The bush pigs, being mostly nocturnal, laid up during the day in the cool, thick grass. We stood in the bed of the safari truck, peering down while the vehicle pushed through the grass. When startled out of their beds, the animals ran fast, and offered little opportunity for shooting. It took several attempts before we took our pigs.

Early in the morning on day three (my bags and guns had arrived the night before), Arwie and J. D. spent some time flying aboard the Cessna, locating buffalo. After the animals were sighted, they GPSed the location of the herd so that we would all have some idea as to where to start looking once we were deep in the swamps. By the time they were back on the ground, our gear

From Dawn Until Dusk

An Argo amphibious vehicle is often the best way to navigate the thick swamps of Mozambique.

was loaded on trucks and trailers for a two-or-three day stint in spike camp.

The trailers carried the Argo amphibious vehicles as well as most of the camping gear. Our camp would consist of dome tents and sleeping bag pads. Not as primitive as backpack hunting in Alaska but not as nice as our base camp, either.

As we neared our final camping spot we moved from dense forest into a flood-plain transition between forest and swamp. The open grass, shallow pans, and clumps of stunted palm trees hid sables, eland, and Liechtenstein's hartebeest, as well as reed buck, oribi, bush pig, and the omnipresent warthogs. By noon the temperature was in the mid-nineties.

Not far from camp, we spotted a herd of hartebeest about five hundred yards away. We stopped to glass the herd. Out of a group of twelve to fifteen, one bull was respectable.

Arwie and J. D. went on to set up camp while Dad, Glen, and I planned a stalk on the bull. Glen led the procession with me following. Dad and Mazua, the head tracker, followed up. Glen carried the shooting sticks. We moved from palmetto to palm tree, trying to keep to as much cover as possible. The sun beat down on us. Each time we reached a new cover point, the shade was as valuable as the cover. As we closed the distance, a large reed buck ram jumped out from a clump of grass. Two more steps and a group of warthogs flushed. We were about two hundred yards from the herd when Glen put the sticks up, the signal for me to get ready. I topped the sticks with my rifle and scanned the herd with the crosshairs, picking out the bull. When I fired. The bullet made a satisfying *whump*.

Right after the shot, I heard a commotion behind me; a few yells, some grunts, and then laughter. I concentrated on the hartebeest and pushed another round into the chamber. Only later did I find out that my shot had jumped another herd of warthogs, and my dad had been charged by one of the boars. Dad had jumped out of the way and was not hurt, but the trackers got a good laugh from this small bit of excitement.

The cows moved off in their typical broken-legged gait. We moved in and gave the bull a finishing shot. The kadonga was down for good.

The fourth day dawned with a thick mist on the ground. We drove deeper into the swamp, the two Argos behind us on trailers. A few miles from spike camp the road dwindled to a rumor, then disappeared entirely. We off-loaded the Argos and put a few provisions on board. Arwie, J. D., and Johnnie the tracker were in one of the eight-wheeled, tracked vehicles while I was in the other with Glen, Dad, and Mazua. Steered only by braking one track or the other, and with no suspension, every bump of an Argo was felt down to the bones.

We headed east further into the Marrameau Swamp, a vast inland delta of the Zambezi River. It had once held huge numbers of buffalo, but as many as fifty thousand a year had been killed during the war. It was only now, years later, that the buffalo had recovered to the point where they could be hunted for sport.

As we entered the swamp proper, the "ground" ahead of us rolled away in waves. What appeared to be solid footing was nothing more than a floating mat of reeds, grass, and papyrus stems. Over the eons, the vegetation had congealed into a two-

From Dawn Until Dusk

foot-thick bio mass. Below this was anywhere from a few inches to several feet of water. A semi-solid muddy bottom greeted one's feet if you fell through the first layer. The two Argos pushed forward for over three hours before we were in good buffalo country. Pods of hippo began appearing in some of the larger pools, and herds of waterbuck dotted the dry patches.

We had agreed that J. D. would have first refusal on buffalo. As we slowed our Argos, Awie and J. D. took the lead. We glassed several locations looking for either buffalo or the tell-tale sign of egrets rising and diving over a herd. We spotted a flock of white birds first, and then saw a black line on the horizon. Buffalo. A good-sized herd a half mile or so away.

While the guides maneuvered the Argos in their direction, a lone bull stood up from the grass about 150 yards away. He looked in our direction, trying to decide if we were something he needed to worry about. He eventually moved off in a jolting lope. Arwie and J. D. climbed from the Argo while their tracker, Johnnie, grabbed the sticks. The buff moved out of sight around a papyrus thicket. J. D. and Arwie followed. Dad and I waited. After a few tense, quiet minutes, the .416 bellowed, followed immediately by the thwack of the bullet's impact. A good hit. There were two more shots. We knew the bull would be down.

Leaving J. D. to his buffalo, we slowly churned forward on our Argo. Within just a few minutes, we had passed a pair of "dugga boys" lying in the deep grass. Dad and I hadn't seen them, but after we were well clear, Glen stopped the Argo and told us what had happened. We readied our guns, jumped out, and circled back, closing the distance to thirty yards before the first bull stood and gave us a glaring look. His horns were small, but he was still big enough to do plenty of damage, and close enough to charge if he had a mind too. I whispered, "No," and shouldered my rifle in a defensive position. He turned away from us, trotting into the enveloping grass. A second bull stood and followed him into green sea. This second bull was much better, but did not wait around to give us a shot.

We returned to the Argo and went another half mile before spotting a second herd on the horizon. We began our stalk. The sparse, intermittent cover forced a crawling, crouching approach. The crust of living material gave way beneath us from time to

Given the danger and effort of the hunt, a Cape buffalo is one of Africa's most prized trophies.

time, dropping us down into the muck, often to our armpits. It was a struggle to keep quiet and hold our guns above the water. We were all soaked through by the time we had pulled ourselves out onto the muddy strip of land on which the buffalo were grazing.

We glassed the herd while Dad readied himself for the shot. Four bulls had pulled away and were starting the move out. The cows began to get nervous. It was only a matter of seconds before they all were going to get the clue. As the bulls slowed to a stop, Dad put a good shot right into the shoulder of the biggest one. A resounding whump, and it was all over.

Dad and I quickly switched rifle and camera. The herd came together and ran another fifty or sixty yards before milling to a stop. I stuffed three more shells into the rifle's magazine.

With binoculars raised to his face, Glen tried to talk me into a bull in the middle of the herd.

"What about that one on the end?" I whispered, looking over the bulls through my scope.

"Yes, that one. He's a good one."

From Dawn Until Dusk

He didn't need to tell me to shoot. A split second later the rifle kicked, and the bull bucked. A second shot also found its way home. The third missed. The bull switched ends, then stood and looked at us broadside. The fourth shot hit with a sound like a large rock dropped into deep water. The bull collapsed. I let out a war whoop and felt a surge of adrenaline.

Dad's bull was not quite dead. We approached him with caution, safeties off, guns ready. Once we were within twenty yards, Glen graciously offered me his Westley-Richards .450 double. I promptly and ingloriously put a bullet into the mud just shy of the bull. Dad then handed me the .458 Lott and I ended the bull's life.

Heading back toward J. D. and Awie, the Argo sank lower in the water. We met our friends as planned, and were soon shaking hands and congratulating each other. A couple hours had passed since J. D. had killed his bull, but vultures had already reduced the animal's carcass to white bones.

We spent that night in spike camp, and moved to base camp the next morning. Glen, Dad, and I went first, and it wasn't long before we spotted two native men sprinting away through the trees. Glen quickly caught up to them, holding them at gunpoint while Jaquime, our second tracker, put handcuffs on them. (He'd been carrying the cuffs the whole hunt, and I had often wondered what he planned to do with them.) The two poachers, young men in their late twenties, led us back to their camp. We then apprehended three of their companions. These men had killed and butchered several warthogs, and were in the process of smoking the meat for sale in the local market. The men also had a number of snares made from bicycle cable. In the process of taking the poachers back to base camp, all five of them managed to escape. I don't think it was ever in the plan to do something with these men. It would have been more trouble than it was worth. Give them a little bit of a scare and then let them escape.

The rest of the hunt was successful in any number of ways. We spent three or four days hunting various species of antelope and pig. I killed a red duiker, two suni (both record-class rams), a nice chobe bushbuck, and a couple of bushpigs. Dad shot a beautiful nyala with finely polished ivory tips. As we stood admiring the nyala in the gathering night, one of the trackers muttered a few

Few antelope in African are as beautiful as the elusive and nocturnal nyala.

---

words and pointed into the forest. Glen looked up from the nyala and whispered, "Elephant."

The weather soon turned for the worse, giving us heavy afternoon rains and high winds. The conditions were poor for nyala, the species, after buffalo, which I most wanted to take. We would see no more nyala this trip. Despite myself, despite our successes, I was a little discouraged. Not even the fresh lion tracks or elephant sign cheered me up.

The hunt ended uneventfully. We spent a final evening around the campfire, sharing stories, polishing up the best parts to retell at home. The next day we flew in the Cessna back to Biera, and from there to Johannesburg.

It wasn't long before we were firmly back in the clutches of civilization. Unlike many hunts in the past, I wasn't really ready to come home. I missed my family, but if I'd had them with me I need not have returned at all. The thrill of hunting dangerous game is addictive.

Chapter 23

Montana Horns

by Allen Morris Jones

It's a tough thing to figure out why it's such a big deal. Sheep hunting.

Every North American game species maintains its own mythology. New Mexico has its elk, Alberta has whitetail, Alaska grows caribou. But for the last few years, there has been no creature more mythic than the Montana bighorn, standing at the precise confluence of genetics and habitat that grows huge rams. In 1970 Montana produced two record-book sheep. In 1995 there were twenty-six. With rumors of a new world-record floating around, Montana's statewide governor's permit has, for the past several years, been auctioned off on both sides of $300,000. The outfitters who guide these hunters end up revolving their careers around the sport.

Here are these animals, 350 pounds of brown against brown hillsides, living in the most unlikely country. If you see them at all, running away, strung out and clattering over broken hillsides, all you find yourself looking at are the horns: horns that curve off their heads like graceful chunks of railroad tie. This is an animal you have to hunt.

For most of us, the only chance at these extraordinary rams is through permit applications. In 1996, when I was twenty-six years old, there was about a 1.5 percent chance that I would draw a tag in Area 124, east of Paradise, Montana. Within my immediate family, among the four of us, there's been a total of nearly one hundred years of applications. It seems, in some ways, unfair that with only fourteen years under my belt it was my license that arrived in the mail.

Area 124 is one of the smallest in the state. Twelve miles long by seven miles wide. In 1996 twenty-two either-sex permits were shoved into this little bean-shaped chunk of Montana, most of it private and unhuntable. Of the public ground, the best sheep country faces south: open shoulders of scrub pine, scarred slides of shale, dark pockets of juniper. The stark hillsides jut four thousand feet up from the banks of the Flathead and Clark's Fork Rivers in a series of scalloped drainages, all of them spread with enough rough fescue—butter on bread for sheep—to make it legitimate big ram habitat.

I decided early on not to hire an outfitter. I wanted to hunt through an area that was still relatively new to my own experience. I wanted to establish an accord with the sheep I killed, uninterrupted by guides or checkbooks. I wanted to *hunt*, without any real concern for record books or point systems.

The day before the season, my father and I stood around a damp fire, shoulders hunched again a cold, mid-September drizzle, trying to keep our spirits up. We stood with his old hunting buddy Ron, watching pickups file into our hunting area. Until just that afternoon, we'd had the place to ourselves, and had been feeling good about things: the way you feel when you've been telling old hunting stories, and looking forward to possibility of new ones.

But by seven o'clock that night our camp had become some kind of social hub for the new hunters. A mechanic from Kalispell, slim and quiet behind his beard, carried a bow. That morning he had scouted the edge of the Flathead Indian reservation to the east and spotted three rams that would all score in the 190s. They were, of course, inside the reservation. A college student from

From Dawn Until Dusk

Missoula, overweight after too many late-night burgers, struggled up the short hill between our campsites and announced that he was a professional hunting guide and was only going to shoot a ram over 200 points, or 180 with his bow. He hitched up his pants. Ten minutes later, a Dodge pickup pulled in, diesel engine clattering. An old guy with dark prescription glasses leaned out the window. "Seen much?"

"Not much. You?"

"Small rams in the bottom."

His wife was a cardigan-wrapped shadow in the front seat beside him. After they left, someone said, "Guess which one drew the tag."

Sheep hunting has somehow managed to bring out both the best and the worst in sportsmen. The Foundation for North American Wild Sheep is one of the finest environmental and sporting groups in the world. With only seven full-time administrators, they have directed more than twenty million dollars to causes benefiting wild sheep: habitat restoration, transplant programs, and water development.

At the same time, trophy sheep have too often been used as a kind of ego rehabilitation. The good idea of a Grand Slam—pushing yourself to hunt all four of North America's wild sheep—has a history that goes back to 1947 and an article in *True* magazine. Since then, what was mostly a neat way of structuring experiences has evolved into occasionally senseless quests for trade-show trophies. It's become an industry. Twelve thousand dollar bighorn hunts in Alberta, eight thousand dollar Dall sheep hunts in Alaska and the Northwest Territories, sixty thousand dollar desert bighorn hunts in Mexico. Fortunately there are these drawn permits: Seventy-eight bucks and lottery-ticket luck.

The language around our campfire that night revolved around numbers. One-nineties. One-eighties. One-eighty-five. I found myself evaluating each of these guys in terms of competition. Once I realized it, I was ashamed of it. Still, nobody really seemed much of a threat, except for the archery guy who was, after all, an archery guy.

A good hunt, I kept telling myself. *A good hunt's all I need.*

Forget points, forget competition. *The hell with it.* Nevertheless, when the fat kid asked me what I was looking for, I said automatically, "One-eighty-five." He looked smug.

Montana's sheep began making news in the early 1970s with transplants from the Sun River. These sheep bloomed into their new habitat, experiencing a grace period of low population and unexploited environment. By 1979 an introduction from Montana's Wild Horse Island was made into the mountains near Perma and Paradise (what would become area 124 thirteen years later). By 1990 that population was estimated at just under 350 sheep. By 1996 a Thompson Falls biologist thought there were at least 550 animals. We had heard rumors of a fifty-inch ram that some outfitters were calling The Snail, due to his unbroomed, twisting curls of horn. Jack Atcheson Jr., one of the better sheep hunters in Montana, had seen him a few times and thought he was too light-horned to go better than 195. But still . . . fifty inches.

After two recent days of scouting, we had seen twenty-one young rams: chewing their cud, digging out beds, kicking forelegs. None of them would score better than the mid-170s.

So. Did we go after the largest of these sheep, hoping that it would grow a few inches in the six hours until dawn, or try somewhere else? Except there was nowhere else. There were supposed to be sheep over the mountain in McLaughlin Creek, but that was mostly private ground: tiny slices of land owned by ex-hippies, broken-down cowboys, and shaved-head militants, all with no-trespassing signs and mean dogs on chains.

We elected to keep close to the group of rams we had spotted. There might be a larger ram we hadn't seen. Play it by ear, we thought.

It was raining when we left camp, the kind of slow, wet drizzle that socks in over a mountain and stays. Dad, Ron, and I began hunting through the timber to the lower slopes, slapping our way through a thicket of wet branches.

An hour later I lay stretched out on an old logging road, staring up at a group of five rams. Through the scope, I could make out the largest of the bunch. After studying him for a few minutes, I

From Dawn Until Dusk

turned to Dad and whispered, "I don't think so." But then I found myself turning back to the scope and reconsidering. The ram that I had almost started to think of as *my* ram wrinkled his nose and tilted it into a light breeze.

And I thought: *This is why you trophy hunt*. Forcing yourself to spend another few days, months, or years on the mountain. But what if there *was* nothing bigger. What if this one was larger than we thought? Sheep are tough to judge. They're scored based on the length of each horn and the circumference at four quarters, with differences in the quarters being deducted from the total. You find yourself making decisions based on length: How loose is the curl, and how heavily are the horns broomed? Without a few years of experience, circumference is mostly something for the tape measure and the corner bar. "Swear to god, thing was *this* big around."

But then the decision was taken out of my hands. The rams were running, the biggest one out first: horns over the hill. There was a rifle shot, just right there.

Dad and I stood up, stretching, looking at each other. I ratcheted a bullet out of the chamber. Twenty minutes later, we set up the spotting scope and watched as a hunter with a ponytail and cowboy hat posed for his own camera, punching the timer before running back to a clump of sagebrush. Through the limbs, we could just make the splayed legs, the tilted horns, of that largest ram.

Before we made it back into camp, we heard five more shots.

According to our topo maps, there was, across the valley, an elbow of private land that cut off easy access to a much larger chunk of public ground below it: A sloping, timbered ridge broken by cliffs and bands of shale. To hunt that brief ridge, we would first have to hike to the bottom of the drainage, skirt the private land, and climb the ridge again. With any luck, this extra two hours of hiking would eliminate the competition.

By the time we were back up on the ridge, it was raining hard. Pounding down. We took cover beneath an enormous fir, leaning back against our packframes and passing a few, softly-spoken words. Twenty minutes later it was still raining and had grown noticeably colder. "Sheep hunting," I said to Ron, "is not all it's cracked up to be."

We snugged up our raincoats and crawled out from under the tree. Dad walked ahead. Dejected but trying to put a face on it, I found myself at the end of the line, peeling a candy bar.

Ten yards ahead, Dad stopped and stood straight, pulling out his binoculars. He sighted down through a jumbled mass of timber and shale. With his free hand, he waved me up. Pulling the rifle off my shoulder, I whispered, "What is it?"

He pointed with his binoculars down the hill, hissing, "Shoot the one on the left."

I looked through my own binoculars and saw two rams staring precisely up at us, motionless in the rain and the rain-fog off the trees. A step or two to the right or left and they would have been invisible. The one on the left was slightly larger—slightly heavier and longer—but they both looked to be record-book sheep. Under their horns, even their bodies were remarkable: the rolling heft and weight of their chests. At 150 yards, this was as close as we'd been to any of the rams we had seen. There was no thought of mental scorecards. Just . . . shoot.

I lowered myself onto my stomach until I was out of their line of vision, and shimmied through wet grass to a pile of rocks just at the edge of our ridge. I tried to rest my gun on the rocks. No good. I stacked the rocks up. Again, no good. The sheep stayed frozen below me, sure they were hidden. Wincing at the amount of movement I was about to make, I took off my jacket and wadded it up into a ball.

I aimed at the base of the larger ram's neck, slightly off-center (shooting downhill, quartering away), held my breath, and squeezed.

And it jumped out of sight. One great leap and he was gone. Maybe, just maybe, he had stumbled. Maybe I was seeing things. Farther around the slope, rocks clattered and rolled.

I lunged up, sliding down the hill on one hip. On the next-lowest knoll, I stood breathing. Two hundred yards out, four rams disappeared over the ridge, bobbing under the weight of their horns. A moment later, except for my breathing, except for the light tap of rain against my hat brim, it was so quiet.

None of the rams had limped, not one had lagged behind.

From Dawn Until Dusk

Drawing a prized bighorn tag was only the start of Allen's run of good luck.

Within that bunch, Ron, from the top of the hill, had glimpsed a ram that he would later swear was at least forty-eight inches: a curl and a quarter, tips spreading away. The Snail.

Dad and Ron stood above me. I yelled up, "Did I get him?"

"I don't think so," Ron said.

"I think I might have seen him go down," Dad said. "Just for a second there. He might have kicked himself on down the hill."

But I had that sick feeling that comes from knowing that things aren't going to turn out right.

Ron stayed up high, shouting down directions, guiding us to where the rams had been when I shot. Dad and I made our way around the hill, fifty or sixty yards apart: a skirmish line in the rain.

Our voices echoed off sheepless hillsides. "Are we there yet?"

"Keep going. To your left."

Almost an hour later, Dad called around the hillside to me. "I think I see him."

My stomach surged and there was suddenly justice in the world. A moment later, Dad yelled out to no one in particular, "Damn, what a ram!"

He lay crooked on the hillside, hooked by his horns against the brush. I leaned my rifle against a boulder and came up to him slowly, sliding a bit and knocking my elbow against the rocks.

In my hands his horns were wet and cold, heavy; his neck hingeless and loose. I smoothed the hair back from my shot, just at the juncture of neck and shoulder. An arrested piece of energy, caught for a moment. But caught only until we could fry up a piece of tenderloin that evening.

We were all suddenly aware of our own slow breaths, the smiles tinged with regret. There was all this sudden loss of potential. Potential swapped for its correlatives: stillness and sadness and a bit of awe. He was so beautiful.

Although it finally wasn't what the hunt was about, wasn't why I was there, we did measure the horns that evening. Forty-two inches on the longest horn. Seventeen-inch bases. A green score of 191 and change. Six-and-a-half years old. By all accounts, the largest ram taken out of 124 that year.

The question *why*, I decided, was finally answered by the experience itself, by the animal.

After the state biologist has pounded a lead plug into the back of one horn, after you've had a shower in some small, moldy hotel room, only then does the reality of what you've just done begin to sink in. Driving back to town, you begin that transition from those most essential things (walking, scanning the hills for the shine of a horn, anticipating the stalk of a remarkable animal) back to radios and tired high school girls at drive-through windows.

It's only at that point that you realize how much of the mountain you've taken away with you, and how much of yourself you've left behind.

Acknowledgments

So many people have contributed to my life (and therefore, the writing of this book), that it would be impossible to recognize them all.

My dad, Opa Jones, instilled in me an excitement and enthusiasm for the hunt—and for so many other things that have directed my life.

In junior high and high school, I shared that excitement with my hunting buddies and with my brother, Glen, who always had a good beagle to help us chase rabbits.

College found me spending time with other fellow enthusiasts—especially my first roommate, Judd, with whom I fished and hunted at every opportunity. My second roommate and lifelong friend Dave Santrock gave me direction in academics and the fine art of fishing—and contributed the photo of me on the cover of this book (thanks again, Dave). In dental school, several of my cohorts became great fishing and hunting partners, folks like Ed Watson, Ernie Shaw, Ken Albinder, and Lyle Wilkinson. Of this group, Ray McCutcheon and Ron Thompson became lifelong buddies, and have shared many of my adventures. My wife, Euni, has been beside me at every step, sometimes hunting with me but always encouraging me to follow my dreams.

Finally, and most importantly, my sons Mark and Allen ...

We have traveled the world together and shared adventures and love far beyond what any of us should have had the right to expect. They have come to know the same excitement that my father instilled in me, and to carry on the same tradition of respect and admiration for the wildlife of the world.

Without Allen and his expertise as writer, editor, and publisher, this volume would not have been possible. He worked on each of these stories, some of which I began writing over thirty years ago.

Thanks, Allen. Over and over.

www.ingramcontent.com/pod-product-compliance
Lightning Source LLC
Chambersburg PA
CBHW071708090426
42738CB00009B/1709